Case   7.5

D0341275

The Sunset Farms Cookbook

The Sunset Farms Cookbook

Rubye Alley Bumgarner

JOHN F. BLAIR, PUBLISHER
WINSTON-SALEM, NORTH CAROLINA

Revised Edition 1991

This book is printed on acid-free paper.

Library of Congress Cataloging-in-Publication Data

Bumgarner, Rubye Alley.
The Sunset Farms cookbook / Rubye Alley Bumgarner.
p.   cm.
Includes index.
ISBN 0-89587-085-1 (alk. paper)
1. Sunset Farms. 2. Cookery, American.   I. Title.
TX715.B9464 1991
641.5973—dc20

91-11118

Contents

ACKNOWLEDGMENTS

To President Edward E. Bryson of Southwestern Technical College for his unending assistance, his interest and confidence in me, I owe my sincere thanks.

To Dr. Sara Sutton Madison, who introduced my "story cookbook" to Chancellor Robinson, and to Director of Public Information, Mr. Doug Reed, who has given his time and know-how to find a publisher; to my good friend, Pat Hill, Senior Vice President of Griswold-Eshlemon Co., who introduced my book to so many; and to Mr. Bill Wright, of *State* Magazine, for his beautiful words of encouragement and help, I wish to say without your help this book would never have been published. Thank you.

To my sister, Edith Alley, for constant encouragement, running errands and helping my good friend and neighbor, Carmen Allison, with proofreading my book, I can only say a sincere thanks.

To Mrs. Betty Arbaugh, who spent hours typing the manuscript, I am truly grateful.

Finally, to my husband, Ed Bumgarner, who put up with me and suggested many incidents in the book, and who encouraged me to make it a reality, I am profoundly grateful.

TO MY PARENTS:
A TRIBUTE

At one time, when newly married, my father and mother lived in a one-room cabin in Whiteside Cove near where my father was born and raised. One day my father had butchered a hog and had put it in a lean-to to work it up the next morning. My mother was quite young and hesitated to tell my father she was beginning to have labor pains, that she knew her first child was going to be born. Finally, although she knew my father was a very tired man, she had to tell him the pains were coming more often. He had to leave her and go by horseback to Cashiers for a midwife to take care of my mother. Cashiers was eight miles away, but he ran his horse to get there, to get the woman on the horse behind him and to hurry back.

In the meantime, my mother told us, a bear came and climbed, growled and scratched at the walls of the house and lean-to trying to get in to the freshly killed hog. She was almost frightened to death. After my father finally arrived with the midwife my brother had already been born. The kind woman was able to give my mother and her little son the care they needed to survive. The nearest doctor was 36 miles away. It was after this horrible experience that my father moved his little family to Cullowhee. This is where the rest of their children were born and raised. At least they lived where they could get a doctor as quickly as he got the original midwife.

This was still a hard life for them. Besides extensive farming, my father was the first person I can recall doing excavating on a large scale. He had no mechanical equipment. However, he used men, several teams of mules and large scrapers that were pulled by mule power. He and his men did a lot of hand work with picks and shovels and wheelbarrows. He excavated the sites for all the first buildings of Western Carolina University, as well as many other public buildings.

This gives an idea of the hard existence my parents had rearing and educating six children.

In this book I will give some of the recipes my mother used when she had the preacher, the teacher or other VIP's to dinner, as well as some of the recipes she cooked just for the family. I hope these recipes will come to mean as much to you as they do to me.

INTRODUCTION

The different seasons of the year have played distinct parts in our lives, so in this book I have tried to convey the joy, the beauty, the trials and hardships of each season, along with the persons who have helped me to apply myself to these circumstances. I've used the good, the odd and the amusing characters who have played so great a part in my life.

America is a land where cultures merge from one generation into the next, and where women continue to take pride in preserving the traditions of the past. They store away yellowed pages of recipes from generation to generation.

I have lived in close contact with the American Indian. Theirs was our first cuisine and was based on wild game, fish, corn and berries. Later they cultivated corn, sweet potatoes and squash and domesticated the wild turkey. Their recipes, too, have been handed down and revised— but still they are the original.

When we pick the beautiful vegetables which we have watched uncurl from the seed, and which we have carefully cared for until they became of edible size, we sometimes wonder, do they compare with those we find that have nature's perfection, such as the tangy dandelion greens, the cresses or wild asparagus—all grown in God's own organic garden without aid of man? Maybe I have a streak of the primitive in me, but from childhood until now I have enjoyed gathering and preparing plant food. I've always been intrigued with the idea of garnering my food from the fields and byways.

Some of the recipes in this book are so rich and full of calories, you will know at once I love men and like to cater to them. Too, some are closely related to health and diet foods, but I feel they are nutritious and have plenty of the right amounts of vitamins, minerals, proteins, carbohydrates and fats.

I believe the food prepared with love and shared with joy is more essential to health than all the vitamins and minerals you find in this book.

This cookbook is the product of many years of labor, an effort that meant years of toil and at the same time, much satisfaction. Through the operation of a mountain inn, we have been rewarded not only by a fairly comfortable living but by making the most wonderful friends from the four corners of the world and from every walk of life. This really began by necessity. Maybe it would be best to say this inn was the product of the great Depression . . . or was it a few chickens?

The Sunset Farms Cookbook

CHICKEN . . .
CHICKEN . . .
CHICKEN . . .

It was our good fortune to marry and to settle on a beautiful knoll at the foothills of the Great Smoky Mountains. It was on that beautiful knoll we learned that we are largely *what* we are partly because we are *where* we are. We had to adapt to our place and to our circumstances.

The small board-and-batten house was entirely hidden from the rest of the world. The joys and hardships we shared in building a way of life were in harmony with the countryside.

Ed was an outdoorsman. We learned to relish the foods we could raise and scavenge from the first days of spring, or from those of a lazy summer. We enjoyed the fruits of cool autumn evenings and had snowbound wintertime feasts.

The things Ed taught me helped me use the things God gives us, some for pleasure and others for survival. After our long days of labor, sometimes our problems would seem too great to bear; but we could always sit on our lawn and look up at our beautiful Smokies. We found solace in repeating Psalm 121:1, "I will lift up mine eyes unto the hills, from whence cometh my help." Always help was soon with us.

Our parents had been great teachers. They instilled in us

a stick-to-itiveness and taught us to be thankful for every blessing.

It was at this time the great Depression came along. With all our misfortunes, where we lived helped us to make a good, useful life. As we were located only one-fourth of a mile from the only road leading to the Great Smokies, it was possible for us to start our great adventure—or shall I call it our career? This was when good food and drink became an art with us.

Ed raised some spring fryers for the market. He spent untold numbers of hours at night, as well as all of the days, feeding and trying to keep the biddies warm with an improvised stove made from a discarded oil barrel. We had spent every available cent we could get to buy feed for them. Finally they were ready for the market. He had sent for a chicken buyer, who readily came as this was early for fryers. We were elated until the buyer offered us nineteen cents per pound for them. We could not take this for we had much more than that invested in feed as well as the hard work and hours of lost sleep. We would have to keep them somehow to sell for a higher price.

I was then teaching school, and God being with us, my month was up and I had a payday and was able to buy some feed for the chickens. I taught in a three-teacher school, eight months a year, for $75 per month.

The next buyer who came offered Ed nine cents a pound. That did it! Ed swore he would feed the chickens to his hunting dogs and give them to our friends and neighbors rather than sell them at such a ridiculous price.

After his anger had subsided I begged him to let us sell chicken dinners. He was quite wary of this, but I out-talked him. Many people passed near our driveway each day. Ed found a board already painted white for me to letter the sign, which we put at the entrance to our hillside. We had no money to buy the tiniest can of paint to do the lettering. However, "necessity is the mother of invention," and we did have some black shoe polish! I used this to letter our "Chicken Dinner" sign. Occasionally it had to be relettered after downpours of rain.

A few people came, and they told others. There was no other place for them to eat. When they came it was an occasion with us. We did the very best cooking we could possibly do. Some tourists wished to stay for a few days. We dressed up our two bedrooms (we slept on a pallet in the attic ourselves) and soon we found ourselves in the innkeeping business. At last we were able to hire a professional sign painter to paint our highway sign. Our original sign has a place of honor among our souvenirs.

You may well know we cooked chicken in every conceivable manner. We not only had "Chicken Every Sunday," but we had chicken two times each day! We became connoisseurs of all chicken dishes. Among those we like best are:

Fried Chicken Marinated in Buttermilk
Gingered Chicken
Orange Baked Chicken Breasts with Almonds
Roast Chicken in a Bag with Cornbread Stuffing
Chicken 'n' Dumplings
Hot Chicken Salad
Chicken Squares

Here are the recipes:

Fried Chicken Marinated in Buttermilk _____ Serves 5 - 6

Cut up a 3 to 3½ pound broiler as you would for family use. Cover chicken completely with buttermilk and let stand in refrigerator for 4 hours.

Preheat oven to 350 degrees. In a black iron frying pan, heat enough Crisco to make a depth of about 2 inches. In a paper bag, mix some flour with a little salt and pepper. Take the chicken out of the buttermilk, place in the paper bag 2 or 3 pieces at a time, shake to coat with flour, then place pieces in hot Crisco. Continue until all chicken is fried crisply brown on both sides. Add ½ cup water to pan. Cover pan tightly and put in oven for 40 minutes.

Gingered Chicken _____ Serves 4

2 T. flour
1 t. salt
1 t. paprika
1 t. ginger
1 t. marjoram
1 2½ to 3 lb. chicken, cut up
3 c. olive oil or
1½ c. shortening and 1½ c. butter or margarine
1 clove of garlic, chopped
3 T. butter, melted
2 T. parsley, chopped

Mix first 5 ingredients together and put in a paper bag. Put pieces of chicken in bag and shake well.

Heat oil or shortening-margarine mixture in heavy skillet. Add chicken and keep turning until brown. Cover and cook about 10 minutes. Remove cover and let get crisp another 10 minutes.

Mix garlic, butter and parsley together and pour over chicken just before serving. Good also with sautéed fresh mushrooms.

Roast Chicken in a Bag with Cornbread Stuffing ___Serves 8

**1 5 lb. roasting
  chicken
  (use giblets to
  make broth to use
  in dressing)
1 lemon, halved
¼ c. butter, softened
1½ t. salt
½ t. pepper
Paprika
½ c. cooking oil**

Rinse and dry chicken; rub inside and out with lemon. Combine butter, salt and pepper. Coat chicken with this mixture, covering back slightly. Sprinkle with paprika. Chill. Stuff chicken lightly with the stuffing below. Preheat oven to 325 degrees. Pour oil into a brown paper bag, shaking until bag is well oiled. Put bag in pan; put chicken into bag breast side up. Twist end of bag securely. Cook chicken 4 hours. Do not open bag while cooking.

Cornbread Stuffing _____

Bake a batch of cornbread a day or two before. When you are ready to stuff the chicken, crumble the cornbread in a large bowl along with 4 or 5 slices of stale white bread. Soak this in chicken broth made from the giblets. Add a finely chopped onion and 3 stalks of celery, finely chopped. Season with salt and pepper, a pinch of poultry seasoning and a little chopped parsley. Add 1 cup of creamed corn and beat in 2 eggs. Stuff chicken before placing in bag.

Orange Chicken Breasts with Almonds _____

Use the required number of chicken breasts you will need for your guests. Season with salt and pepper. Brown chicken on both sides in margarine.

Put the browned breasts in a large baking pan. Pour over this 1 can of frozen orange juice mixed with 1 can of water.

Cover and simmer 20 minutes or until tender. Pour liquid into a saucepan and cook until slightly thickened. Then pour back over chicken and sprinkle with toasted almonds.

Chicken 'n' Dumplings _____ Serves 7 - 8

Cut up a 5 pound broiler and cook in enough water to cover plus 2 sticks of margarine, 1 teaspoon salt and ½ teaspoon pepper. Cook slowly until tender. When broth is boiling briskly, drop dumplings in (see recipe below) and boil 10 to 15 minutes.

Dumplings _____

2 c. flour
½ t. salt
4 T. shortening
(Crisco)
⅔ c. milk (about)
2 qts. chicken broth
Black pepper to taste

Combine flour and salt; cut in shortening until of a mealy consistency. Add just enough milk to make a stiff dough. Roll very thin and cut into squares. Drop dumplings a few at a time into boiling broth. Sprinkle with freshly ground pepper. When broth boils over the dumplings, add another layer. Boil 10 to 15 minutes.

Hot Chicken Salad
Serves 4 - 6

1½ c. chopped celery (I like to use the green pascal)
¾ c. sliced toasted almonds
3 c. cooked cubed chicken
¾ t. salt
1½ c. mayonnaise
3 T. lemon juice
1 sm. can of mushrooms, chopped
1½ c. grated sharp cheddar cheese
1½ c. potato chips

Preheat oven to 450 degrees. Combine the first 7 ingredients. Put in a casserole, then cover the top with cheese and potato chips. Bake for 12 minutes.

Chicken Squares _____ Serves 8

4 chicken breasts
2 T. melted
  margarine
8 oz. cream cheese
1/4 t. salt
1/8 t. black pepper
2 T. milk
1 T. minced onion
8 oz. can of Pillsbury
  Refrigerated Quick
  Crescent Rolls
1 can condensed
  cream of chicken
  soup
1/4 cup milk

Stew chicken breasts. After cooking, cut in small pieces. Preheat oven to 350 degrees. Blend cream cheese with margarine until smooth. Add chicken, salt, pepper, milk and onion. Mix well. Separate rolls into triangles. Place a spoonful of chicken mixture into center of each triangle. Roll or fold edges of triangle together and pinch together to seal. Place on ungreased cookie sheet and bake for 20 minutes or until golden brown. Serve with sauce of cream of chicken soup plus 1/4 cup of milk heated to form gravy. Pour over chicken.

SNOW TIME IS
SOUP TIME

Because we desired to please others and to have the wonderful friends we had made keep coming back, we continued our inn long after the original chickens were gone.

One of the first things we learned was that our "boarders" wanted our local food. Therefore, I used my mother's recipes, my sisters' and sisters'-in-law. I used those of other good cooks, my friends and neighbors, my customers and many of my own concoctions, often through necessity.

All the long winter days our thoughts and preparations were for our summer boarders. We would sit and watch the falling snow and try to walk down the icy steps to feed the hundreds of songbirds who had learned they no longer had to be scavengers here!

Wintery days called for a soup pot. When I think of soup I always recall my first effort at cooking. At home my work was outside. My father was almost an invalid. He had to walk with two sticks from a terrible case of arthritis. (Now I'm on one cane plus a steel brace with the same affliction.) My two older brothers had left home to be on their own. My younger brother was almost an invalid with asthma. Therefore, I became my father's helper with the horses, cattle, hogs, etc. This is the reason I'd never learned to cook. But I decided to try to make Ed some soup for our first meal after we were married. I tried. He had worked hard and was a hungry man. When he asked for a second helping and where I got my recipe, I thought he was kidding me. He wasn't! It was then I vowed I'd learn to cook.

I made many attempts before I finally came up with my own "cheese soup" that became nationally known. Soon we realized people were driving two to three hundred miles off their route to buy a bowl of our cheese soup. We used it for a dinner starter. And, too, it became a wonderful luncheon served with two hot popovers and a watercress salad.

I like men and have found myself catering to them for years—maybe it's because they enjoy eating and they don't count calories. This is one reason we served these delicious, creamy, rich soups. The soup pot was always ready for fear of a blizzard or snow storm.

I vividly recall the wonderful soups my mother made. When the snow came, she always had one of her famous pots of soup on the back of the stove. In this she had any leftover meat-bones from roasts or boiled dinners, scraps of meat, leftover potatoes or turnips, a cup or two of tomatoes, any leftover potato water, a chicken carcass already divested of any meat, a bowl of unused gravy and a stalk or two of celery. All went into this simmering pot to make a surprisingly flavorful broth that she strained at suppertime, discarding the bones, etc. Into another kettle this broth was put to start our evening soup, to which she added noodles or dumplings, potatoes, tomatoes or any vegetable, all loaded with vitamins. She added onions, parsley she had dried, two sticks of butter, sometimes a jigger of sherry and a slice of lemon. Into the pot went more water, a leftover veal bone, a chicken wing (left from lunch), plus a few scrubbed yellow chicken feet, perhaps a carrot, sometimes a shin bone or piece of rump from the fall butchering to replenish this magic or famous cauldron for tomorrow. Whether or not one feels uneasy at the antiquity of my mother's soup, don't forget it was always pleasant to walk into her kitchen on a cold, cloudy, bitter day. The warmth and fragrance were always compelling.

Rubye's Cheese Soup — Serves 25

2 qts. of milk
1 qt. of chicken or
   beef broth
3 oz. dark beer
1½ green peppers
1½ carrots
1 stalk of celery
1 med. onion
2 cloves garlic
2 T. melted
   margarine
1³/₅ c. flour
2²/₃ c. grated cheese (I
   use sharp cheddar)

Mix the first 3 ingredients together and let come to a boil. Dice vegetables and garlic and run through the blender with margarine. Add to heated liquids. Then blend in flour and grated cheese and simmer for an hour. This can be stored in the refrigerator for days. We usually served croutons with it, or popovers when it was to be a full luncheon.

Watercress-Potato Soup _____ Serves 10

2 qts. potatoes, thinly
   sliced
2 stalks celery,
   chopped
2 qts. water
1 med. chopped
   onion
1 qt. beef broth
1½ t. salt
½ t. freshly ground
   pepper
3 c. watercress,
   chopped

Combine all ingredients except watercress and let boil until the vegetables can be mashed with a potato masher into a pulp. Add watercress.

To make it have even more calories, we ate this with crumbled corn bread.

Pot "Likker" Made from Cabbage or Spring Greens _____

Cover 1 average size ham hock with water. Add black pepper and 1 small pod of red pepper. Boil meat until tender. Add cabbage or greens. (If I use cabbage, I take the core out, then cut it in four pieces and separate the leaves.) Cook at least an hour, adding water as needed. Strain off the liquid—the pot "likker." Serve in soup bowls and dunk corn bread in it. Be sure not to dunk more than your mouth will hold.

Fresh spring greens make a delicious "likker." Many babies are fed spoonfuls of this and thrive on the vitamins they get.

Cow Pea Soup   Serves 6

2 c. dried cow peas
Water to cover peas
1 ham bone
2 qts. water
1 onion, chopped
½ c. chopped celery
2 t. salt
Pepper to taste
Lemon slices

Cover peas with water and let soak overnight. Next day drain peas, put in a kettle with ham bone, 2 quarts water, onion, celery and salt. Cook until peas are soft. Remove bone and purée soup in blender. Reheat soup; add pepper. Serve in hot soup cups. Garnish each serving with a slice of lemon.

Black-Eyed Peas and Hog Jowl   Serves 10

1 lb. dried black-eyed
  peas
1 4 in. piece of hog
  jowl, sliced
Salt
Water
1 sm. red pepper pod
Worcestershire sauce

Rinse and pick over peas. Cover with water and let soak overnight. Next day, drain peas. Sprinkle the jowl with 3 teaspoon salt and then fry in a skillet until browned. Transfer to a kettle. Add soaked peas plus enough water to cover by 1 inch. Add salt to taste and then red pepper. Bring to a boil. Cover and simmer 3 to 4 hours. Add additional water during cooking if necessary. Add Worcestershire to taste.

Chicken Velvet Soup

Serves 8

2 T. cold milk
2 T. cornstarch
1 qt. chicken stock
1 c. half-and-half
4 egg yolks, beaten
Curry powder
Cayenne pepper
1 t. salt
1/8 t. white pepper
1/4 t. celery salt
1 t. onion juice
whipped cream

Blend milk and cornstarch until smooth, then combine in kettle with stock. Let simmer until it tastes cooked, then add half-and-half and bring mixture to a boil.

Place beaten egg yolks over water in a double boiler; pour stock mixture slowly into egg yolks, beating constantly. Cook over boiling water until eggs are cooked. While mixture is cooking, add a speck of curry and a speck of cayenne, the salt, white pepper, celery salt and onion juice. Serve with a blob of whipped cream on top.

Rich but delicious!

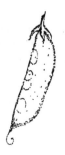

Bean Soup _____ Serves 12

Soak 2 cups white northern beans in water overnight. In the morning drain them and put them to boil in 3 quarts of water along with a ham bone or hock, a handful of celery leaves, a diced carrot, 2 large sliced onions, ¼ teaspoon thyme, ½ teaspoon summer savory and ½ small red pepper pod. Simmer several hours until beans are absolutely tender. Take out bones and meat, then run beans through a sieve. Return pulp to broth. Add salt to taste. Bring to a boil and stir well; add slivers of ham cut from the bone and a few splashes of Madeira, port or sherry, as you like. Serve in a tureen; float on the soup thin slices of lemon and blobs of unsweetened whipped cream, the whole sprinkled liberally with grated yolks of several boiled eggs. This is perfect served with a tart vinaigrette salad along with corn sticks. This makes a man's meal. Forget calories— don't count!

German Potage _____ Serves 10

½ lb. split peas
3 qts. water
1 minced onion
¼ c. chopped celery
2 carrots, sliced
1½ oz. ham bone

Soak peas overnight to soften. Bring peas, onion, celery and carrots to boil in water. Add ham bone and cover. Simmer until peas are tender and partially cooked down (about 1½ hours). Press through sieve or crush in blender until you have a smooth texture. Serve with popped corn or toast points.

Peanut Butter Soup About 12 5-oz. servings

1 c. celery, cubed
1/8 c. onion, chopped
1/8 c. green pepper,
   chopped
1 c. boiling water
1/8 c. all-purpose
   flour
1½ qts. milk, rich
2 c. peanut butter
2 t. sugar
Salt and pepper to
   season

Simmer celery, onion and green pepper in boiling water for 10 minutes Drain, reserving water.

Combine flour with milk and the water in which the vegetables were cooked. Add vegetables, then add peanut butter and sugar. Season with salt and pepper. Blend peanut butter well into mixture. Cook in double boiler or steam jacketed kettle until mixture is well blended and hot. Serve with chopped peanuts or chopped parsley and popped corn. This recipe was given to us by a teacher of Tuskegee Institute in Alabama.

Cream of Spinach Soup _____ Serves 8

1½ lbs. fresh spinach
2 T. butter or
   margarine
½ c. finely chopped
   onion
2 T. flour
Salt and freshly
   ground pepper, to
   taste
4 c. milk or half milk
   and half heavy
   cream
Cayenne pepper to
   taste
Whipped cream to
   garnish

Cook spinach in a covered kettle only in the water left on spinach from washing. Heat the butter in a saucepan and add the onion. Cook onion until wilted. Sprinkle flour, salt and pepper over onion. Add milk, stirring rapidly. Pour this mixture into a blender and add spinach; purée until smooth. Return to saucepan, add cayenne and bring just to boil. Serve hot or cold with a garnish of whipped cream.

THE OPEN FIELDS
AND STREAMS

In addition to our gardening bit, we both loved the out-
doors. Some of our best recipes came from the fields,
woods and streams. Most of these recipes were Ed's.

As the days began to get longer and we saw the swelling
of the buds, we knew winter was finally passing.

I could be house-bound no longer. I got a basket and
sharp-edged knife, and with a glorious feeling, our beautiful dog, Lady, and I started on my pursuit for wild greens.

Those who have not taken a walk through the fields in
the springtime stalking delicious greens have not lived!
You must breathe the pure air, smell the good earth, see
the uncurling of the wonders of nature and taste the delicacies God has given us to have really lived.

Some of the greens my mother taught me to "tell" and
then to cook are sheep sorrel and dandelion. Besides being
edible, these are thought to be a remedy for what ails people in the spring. The dandelion, along with many of the
herbs, has medicinal value. The fresh greens possess a
slight narcotic property. The roots, dried when fresh, are a
stomachic and tonic with a slightly diuretic action. They
have long been used as a home remedy.

We gathered the young blackberry leaves, field and
watercress. Most of the local people call field cress

"creeses." We used the long leaf dock, mouse-ear, poke, plantain and wild lettuce (sometimes called branch lettuce or bear lettuce). Often we thought this last should be named for the ruffed grouse, for they eat and thrive on it. We found and used lamb's-quarters, crow's foot, parslane, wild mustard and, one of my favorites, the wild violet leaves (mix with other greens).

Here are some of our recipes:

Mixed Greens

Use any of the wild greens listed above. (I usually have at least ½ gallon of greens.) Carefully look at greens before wetting them. Try to have about an equal part of each kind. Then wash in at least 4 waters. Let stand in a pan of salty water. This takes any insects out of them. All this time you should be simmering about 3 rashers of salt pork in 2 quarts of water. Then parboil the greens for a few minutes in plain water. Drain in a colander, then place into the salt pork water. Let cook until tender with 1½ teaspoon salt. These may be served as is or with sliced boiled eggs over top. Use vinegar if you wish. But we omit the vinegar with ours. By all means serve cracklin' bread with them if the wind is blowing a little chilly—don't forget the pot likker from this is delectable and is a spring tonic.

Poke "Sallet"

Gather a basket of young poke that is just sticking its head from the ground (these young sprouts remind one of young asparagus). Wash thoroughly. Parboil for about 6 to 8 minutes in a little amount of water. Drain thoroughly. Run a sharp knife through them and chop coarsely—you will find them so tender. Put them back over low heat and season with bacon drippings or butter and salt to taste. Do not add any water.

Poke with Eggs

Use the recipe above to cook poke. After you have cut the boiled poke, drain, put in a fry pan that has 4 table-spoons of hot margarine and to this add 4 beaten eggs. Scramble together with the poke. Serve with hot hoecakes. This makes a luncheon fit for a king.

Sautéed Poke Stalks

Gather 1 quart of young, tender stalks of poke. Wash thoroughly. Cut in 1/2 inch pieces, salt and pepper lightly, then roll in cornmeal. Have your fry pan hot with butter (about 1 stick). Saute poke in butter until golden brown. This reminds one of fried okra—only better.

Creesy Greens (Upland Cress) _____

This is a delicious wild green that has a distinctive peppery flavor all its own. The taste is one that many have to cultivate. No greens can compare with creesy greens. The taste and aroma make this springtime dish truly a delight! Be sure you begin gathering as early as possible as creesy greens become bitter as they grow and begin to form blooms.

Look the greens over well and shake off all trash and dried leaves before putting in water. Leave some of the bunches intact, for the center gives a good flavor. Wash thoroughly through 5 or 6 waters. After you have parboiled the greens, put them in a pot where you already have a ham bone or rasher of salt pork boiling. Salt to taste. Boil until very tender. They are delicious with shallots or chives cut over. By all means serve with corn bread. I suggest my mother's corn pone (see index).

Dandelion Greens _____

In late March or early April the young sheltered plants are the very best, and be sure to use some of the bloom buds that have not burst into bloom. It is quite a chore to pick and clean the greens but be sure to clean them of any trash or grit before wetting. Then parboil for 3 minutes. Wash again. Put in a pot in which you are boiling a sizable piece of sowbelly. Always serve some type of corn bread with them.

The first tender leaves showing after the snows have melted are fantastic in a tossed salad. Other ingredients are hard boiled eggs, finely chopped, and chopped scallions. We use a vinegar and oil dressing—this is delicious!

Violet Jam

Put as many blossoms as you can pack into a 1 cup measure. Put in blender and add ¾ cup water and juice of 1 lemon. Blend till smooth. Slowly add 2½ cups sugar and blend until dissolved. Stir 1 package of powdered pectin and ¾ cup of water together. Add violet mixture from blender. Bring to boil and boil hard 1 minute. Quickly pour into jars and seal. Keeps in refrigerator 3 weeks and in freezer for 6 months.

The springtime taught us the glory of God's creation. Psalm 19, written by David, has been called the greatest of all the Psalms. David was an outdoorsman, as I have spoken of Ed as being. He not only observed nature but also interpreted its meaning.

Ed would talk to me of the brilliant sunrise and the part it played in the creation and beauty around us. Ed had to have some insight into the great solar system that our scientists are delving into today. He always spoke of the sunsets and the rest they offered for all living things. Ed believed the sun and moon played a great part in nature. He believed there was a certain phase of the moon to plant different things.

We went on nature treks together, and many times we were rewarded by finding some of the rare flowers—such as the delicate shortia (almost extinct), the showy orchis, and many other orchids, the phacelia and the painted and yellow trillium. These made a day we could not soon forget.

After a long, wonderful day fishing the clear, sparkling streams, we were always ready for a rest. We fished for trout from these clear, cool waters. We cleaned and cooked them right by the water. Trout have a taste you just don't find in other fish. They are so sweet and fine-grained that an amateur cook would find it hard to spoil this delectable fish. And they have an incomparable delicacy when eaten right after being caught. While Ed made our "Hush Puppies" that he fried in the same fat in which he had fried the fish, I gathered mountain lettuce for our salad. Also, I brought young scallions along to go with it: This is really eating!

For those who do not know the mountain lettuce or ramps, I will try to explain. Each grows only back in the undisturbed places of nature. The lettuce grows among the rocks right in the stream from which we have caught the trout.

Near that stream in a rich woods we find the ramp growing. It belongs to the lily or onion family. Its taste and odor are much stronger than garlic. If you eat it raw, you should plan to stay out of civilization for five or six days. But ramps are delicious fried with potatoes. We also pickle them. When cooked, they don't give you such a strong odor. Here is one recipe for ramps.

Cheese Scalloped Ramps _____ Serves 15

About 1½ qts. of ramps, peeled and cleaned
1 c. ½ in. cubes processed American cheese
8 slices buttered toast
½ c. margarine
½ c. enriched flour
2 c. milk
½ t. salt
¼ t. pepper
8 eggs, beaten

Cook ramps in boiling water until tender, about 10 minutes. Drain well and place half the ramps in 2 quart casserole. Add half of the cheese and half of the toast. Repeat layers of ramps and cheese. Melt margarine, blend in flour and stir in milk gradually. Cook, stirring constantly, until thick. Add salt and pepper. Add a little of this hot mixture to beaten eggs and gradually stir-pour sauce over layers. Top with remaining toast. Bake in 350 degree oven for 30 minutes.

We had a friend who brought us shad and mullet from the Florida shores. These we used to fry, bake, or use for chowder.

Catfish is distinctive in this area. It is small, bony, and abundant. Primarily, it is coated with cornmeal and fried, but it is used to make a catfish stew or even into a delicious salad.

Here are some of our fish recipes, plus those given us by our friends from the seashores.

Baked Seafood Casserole _____ Serves 8

2½ lbs. crabmeat
2½ lbs. shrimp
2½ c. mayonnaise
1¼ c. chopped green
  pepper
⅔ c. chopped onion
3¾ c. chopped celery
1¼ t. salt
2½ T. Worcestershire
5 c. crushed potato
  chips

Combine all ingredients except potato chips and pour into buttered casserole. Top with potato chips. Bake at 250 degrees 25 to 35 minutes.

Mountain Trout _____

Clean and dress trout as they are taken from the stream. Salt lightly, then roll in cornmeal. They are best fried until golden brown in the hot fat where we have fried salt pork (this pork we fed Lady, our bird dog, who went with us everywhere we went). After this we fried the hush puppies and sometimes the potatoes and ramps.

Baked Bass _____

The flavor of bass is so fine they can be baked and served with slices of lemon. However, we like them baked using a little corn bread stuffing seasoned with a little fresh dill. To bake we first scale them, then sprinkle the inside and out with salt and pepper. Brush with melted butter and sprinkle with paprika. Bake on a greased broiler in a 375 degree oven until the fish flakes when tested with a fork.

Baked Shad _____

No fish has a finer flavor than North Carolina shad. Wipe cleaned shad with a damp cloth. Sprinkle inside and out with salt, pepper, and lemon juice. Fold in greased aluminum foil, using 3 layers of heavy thickness. Place on a baking pan and bake at 250 degrees. Bake a 1½ to 2 pound shad for 5 hours. Bake a 2½ to 5 pound fish for 5½ to 6½ hours.

Oyster Stew _____

For 2 servings, cook ½ pint of oysters over low heat in 4 tablespoons butter. Season with salt and pepper, paprika, and a squirt of Lea & Perrins sauce. Sprinkle 2 tablespoons flour over oysters and blend in. Add 2 cups rich milk; heat but don't dare boil. Serve in soup bowls with a small clump of butter on top. Serve hot, of course.

Fish Chowder _____ Serves 6

1 lb. haddock or
  mullet
1 t. salt
1 c. cold water
¼ lb. fatback or salt
  pork, diced
6 sm. potatoes,
  peeled and diced
2 onions, finely
  chopped
2 c. boiling water
1 T. flour
1 pt. milk
1 T. butter
Parsley and paprika

Put fish in cold water, heat to simmering. Cook gently 10 minutes. Remove fish from water, reserving water. Remove skin from fish, return to cooking water.

In a deep, heavy kettle slowly fry fatback or salt pork until crisp. Remove crisp fat and discard. Add potatoes, onions and boiling water. Cover and cook for 10 minutes. Add fish and cover and cook, simmering, for 5 minutes. Stir in a smooth mixture of the flour and milk; bring to a boil. Before serving, add butter, then add parsley and paprika to taste.

Escalloped Oysters ———————————— Serves 4

1 pt. oysters,
  undrained
½ c. soft bread
  crumbs
1 c. cracker crumbs
½ c. melted butter
¼ c. oyster liquor
  (juice from canned
  oysters)
¼ c. cream
Salt and pepper to
  taste

Mix bread and cracker crumbs. Stir in melted butter. Put a thin layer of this mixture in bottom of baking dish. Cover with oysters; sprinkle with salt and coarsely ground pepper. Mix remaining oysters and oyster liquor with the cream and make a second layer with this mixture. Cover top with remaining crumb mixture. Bake about 30 minutes in a hot 450 degree oven. Never use more than two layers of oysters to a pan. If more layers are used the middle layers will not cook sufficiently. This recipe will double or triple in exact proportions for more servings.

Do not add other seasoning. This simple recipe compliments the flavor of the delicate, succulent oyster.

Pickled Shrimp _____ Serves 6

2 qts. Wesson Oil
1 qt. vinegar
1 12 oz. bottle wine
  vinegar
1 pkg. pickling spice
2 14 oz. bottles
  catsup
1 6 oz. jar prepared
  mustard
1 5-oz. bottle soy
  sauce
1 Mexican pepper
1 10-oz. bottle Lea &
  Perrins sauce
2 chopped cloves
  garlic
2 large chopped
  onions
10 lbs. shrimp

Mix thoroughly all ingredients except shrimp. Divide into two large glass jars. Peel shrimp and devein. Cook in salted water. Drain and place in sauce while hot. Refrigerate at least 3 days, stirring occasionally.

I must stop at this point to tell of an incident we had with the great ballad singer, "Singing Sam, the Barbasol Man." He and another young man came to our place to go on a trip fishing for mountain trout. Their wearing apparel looked more as if they were ready for a masquerade. Their hats were covered with artificial flies. They wore waist-deep waders and Bowie knives strapped to their belts. They really were dressed for their fishing trip as they thought they should be.

Ed had a guide we shall call Mac to direct these trips. Ed

could not resist going this time. Mac also expected a good time of it. Our cook, Charlotte, also went along.

Soon they were packed and ready to go. Ed and Mac were carrying only their cheap rods and reels. Their guests were loaded with $65 rods and nets.

Ed took them to a fine fishing stream in the Smokies where it was most likely they would catch their limit quickly.

The men could hardly wait to hit the stream. The water was as clear as crystal and looked to be five or six inches deep. Ed got a good laugh when the younger man, with his waders, stepped into a pool of water and found it to be about waist deep. Singing Sam and his friend found they had the wrong waders. You must have cleats or felt soles to wade on those scum-covered rocks.

Finally the younger man called, "Mac, come quickly! Come!" When Mac reached the man he had a trout about three inches long attached to the end of his rod. He called, "I've caught one! Now, Mr. Mac, what do I do next?" His rod was sticking straight up and he was looking up at it. Very disgustedly Mac called, "Climb your rod, get your Bowie knife, and stick him."

However, Ed and Mac soon had the limit for four and the men were ready to call it quits. I think they had a meal they wouldn't soon forget. Charlotte was an artist with trout. After the trout were thoroughly scraped she shook them in a paper bag with meal and salt and pepper and dropped them in her hot Crisco for about one minute on each side. Then she served them garnished with parsley and hush puppies.

Here is her recipe for hush puppies. These are truly the greatest.

———————————

Charlotte's Hush Puppies _____ Serves 8

3 c. cornmeal
1 t. salt
¹/₂ t. black pepper
1 large yellow mild
  onion, chopped
  fine
1 egg
4 T. cooking oil
1¹/₂ t. baking powder
Milk

Mix cornmeal, salt, pepper and onion. Stir in egg, oil and baking powder. Stir in enough milk to hold the mixture together. Shape into small finger size pones and fry in skillet with fish.

Ed thoroughly enjoyed going on the trips with Singing Sam and a great number of our other guests. However, he was happier with the friends described in the following verse, which was written by a man he loved and admired. Fred was a newspaper reporter who was very close to us. He lived in Indiana, but when he was told he had only two months to live he came back to stay with us until the end—which came in three and a half weeks. Tom was a grand old Englishman who spent many summers with us.

This verse is set in our beautiful Blue Ridge Mountains—he speaks of "Silver Run." It is a crystal-clear stream.

A Truthful Tale
By M. Y. Jarrett

Upon a lovely summer day
We four met on the broad highway
And there agreed to seek for fun
By chasing trout in Silver Run.

The first was Ed, a mountain youth
An earnest seeker after Truth (He hasn't
    found it yet)
Who dug the bait and led the way
Just at the breaking of the day.

The next was Tom, a tourist he,
Who from the Southland heat did flee
He deals in badly used up cars
And sings, off-key, a few sad bars.

The next was Fred, who writes the news
And tells us everything that brews
You can believe whate'er he'll say
(We tried him out that summer day).

The last was I, to fame unknown
Who writes this story all alone
And try to tell just what occurred
And hereby vouch for every word.

We fished and fished the live long day
And all the big fish got away
(At least that's what Tom told his wife
To thus prevent domestic strife).

We fished with bait, we fished with fly
We cast 'em low, and we cast them high

Some hit the water, some the trees
And some waved idly in the breeze.

Each fish disdained our every snare,
He'd look at us and coldly stare,
Then thumb his nose at us and wink
(It almost drove poor Tom to drink).

The burning sun above looked down
And in derision seemed to frown
Upon our efforts all so vain
(Such fishing just gives me a pain).

Then when the sun shot his last beam
And darkness fell upon the stream
The screech owl's weird and ghostly call
From out the pine trees seemed to fall.

Then by a campfire's cheerful gleam
We gathered there beside the stream
And many a fancy tale was spun
Beside the waves of Silver Run.

A question rose, I know not why
Of who could tell the biggest lie
And soon a contest was begun
Above the falls of Silver Run.

Being a truthful person, I,
Like Cherry George could tell no lie,
And 'twas agreed that I must say
Who won the prize upon that day.

For he who told the strangest tale
Should win a case of gingerale
(It should be bought with his own pelf
I care for no such prize myself).

Ed started in and I tell you
That half his lies were just not true
His lying was so very poor
'Twas plain he was an amateur.

But Frederick, now, 'twas plain that he
Had lied by land and lied by sea,
He lied of fish, he lied of whales,
He lied of storms, he lied of gales.

He lied of snakes, he lied of trees,
He lied of kings and bumble bees.
So smoothly ran his every tale
It looked as tho' he'd win the ale.

But Tom was a courageous man
Where others stopped, he just began
With stony eye and solemn face
He lied with art, he lied with grace.

Each lie he told I felt was true
And had you been there so would you,
He told such plain and fancy lies
I gladly yielded him the prize.

But I am sure I'll not again
Seek sport with such ungodly men
Who deal so lightly with the truth
And oft beguile the trusting youth.

As around the campfire's fitful gleam
They smoke and lie and nod and dream
Of speckled trout that weigh a ton
Below the falls of Silver Run.

Despite Mr. Jarrett's tale he so nicely spun, Ed came home with his creel full of trout.

RECIPES FROM
OUR GARDEN

As winter went on we pored over our piles of seed catalogues and thrilled over the luscious-looking vegetables and the colorful flowers. It was then we gave thanks for the seed catalogues, but we stopped and wondered how long we would have to wait for spring. It was so hard for us to realize we couldn't plant and cultivate half the seeds we wished to order. Always we bought more than we had room to plant or time to harvest.

We never forgot there is something about digging in the good earth that heals the soul. It is such a rewarding experience to see the tiny plants emerge and grow into delectable food.

Ed and I found gardening a real labor. But let me say now it was a labor of love. From our tremendous gardens we grew the food for our summer boarders, and we canned and froze our produce for the coming season. We not only had enough for that but enough to share with the neighbors, who were real neighbors. In sickness, death, and trouble we could depend on them. We found it to be a tiny thing to share with them, but to us sharing was one of God's great blessings, the ultimate way of life.

While I write this cookbook and think back over our works and our friends, I find solace that Ed and I have been a part of so great a country. And don't ever believe we have not been blessed—for I know no two people who ever enjoyed our beautiful country and friends and neighbors more than we have.

Jams, jellies and pickles from our produce were always good to share. Here are some of our favorites:

Corn Cob Jelly

12 corn cobs from which sweet corn has been cut
4 c. water
1 box fruit pectin
4 c. sugar

Boil corn cobs in water 10 minutes, than strain through a cloth for 3 cups of juice. Add enough water to finish the 3 cups if needed. Put juice in a pan, add pectin, bring to boil. Add sugar (all at once) and bring to a rolling boil. Remove from stove, skim, put in jars and seal. This tastes like honey. Add food coloring if you wish.

Grace Rowe's Pepper Jelly

6½ c. sugar
1 c. bell pepper, chopped fine
¾ c. hot pepper, chopped fine
1½ c. cider vinegar
1 6 oz. bottle Certo

Mix sugar, chopped peppers, and vinegar. Bring to a rolling boil and boil 7 minutes. Drain. Add Certo. Take off heat and let stand for about 5 minutes. I add a few drops of food coloring (red or green). Put in sterilized jars and cover with paraffin.

This is great as an appetizer on cream cheese and Triscuits. It may be served with pork or ham at a meal.

Jim Jam Jelly

4 ripe tomatoes
6 tart apples
Sugar
1/2 c. cider vinegar
2 whole cloves
2 whole allspice
1 in. stick cinnamon
1/2 c. raisins, ground

Peel tomatoes and cut in small pieces. Pare apples and cut in small cubes. Measure and add as many cups of sugar as fruit. Place tomatoes, apples and sugar in a kettle. Add vinegar and spices in a bag. Simmer all 1 hour or until thick (watch closely so it does not scorch). Add raisins and simmer a half-hour longer. Remove spices and pour into glasses. Cover with paraffin.

This is very good served with ham.

Tommye's Yellow Cucumber Pickle

7 lbs. cucumbers,
   peeled, seeded and
   sliced
1 gal. water
2 c. lime
3 T. alum
5 lbs. white sugar
1 sm. box pickling
   spice
1 t. salt
3 pints apple vinegar
1 t. turmeric

Mix water, lime and alum; pour over cucumbers and let stand 24 hours. Wash cucumbers in clean water and let sit in clean water 1 hour. Rinse in fresh water 4 times.

Boil remaining ingredients together; pour over cucumbers and let stand 24 hours or longer. Then bring cucumbers and liquid to boil for 15 minutes. Can in sterilized jars.

Capers

For color, flowers, and fragrance we planted long rows of nasturtiums around our garden. For parties I have used the colorful blooms to garnish the iced tea. However, my main purpose in growing so many was to gather the seeds to make into capers. It was easy and no one can tell them from the expensive capers in the market. I carefully sterilized the containers, then filled them with the nasturtium seed. I added ⅛ teaspoon salt to each ½ pint jar and filled the jars with a boiling solution of 1 part water and 1 part vinegar. Then I sealed the jars.

End of Garden Pickles

1 c. sliced cucumber
1 c. chopped sweet
  pepper
1 c. chopped cabbage
1 c. cauliflower,
  broken up
1 c. sliced onions
1 c. chopped green
  tomatoes
1 c. chopped carrots
1 c. cut green beans
1 T. celery seed
1 c. chopped celery
2 c. vinegar
2 c. sugar
2 T. turmeric
2 T. mustard seed

Soak cucumbers, peppers, cabbage, cauliflower, onions and tomatoes in ½ cup salt water overnight. Cook carrots and green beans in boiling water about 10 minutes. Drain well. Mix soaked and cooked vegetables with remaining ingredients and boil 10 minutes. Pack in sterilized jars and seal at once.

You can do wonders with vegetables to keep your guests and family happy. They can be "pepper-uppers" for lagging appetites. For instance, corn is an adaptable vegetable, and its piquant flavor and fresh color help out in adding variety to vegetables. Mixed vegetables of all sorts with a few corn kernels are pretty to look at as well as good to eat.

Slivering vegetables instead of dicing them makes for better flavor, if only psychologically. When dressing up vegetables with the flavor of butter, you might like to add onion, chives, herbs, mint, garlic, curry powder, parsley or watercress, or all sorts of bread or cracker crumbs.

Peas and rice cooked together make a pretty vegetable, and one that is accepted by those who care for neither separately.

Cream never hurt anything but your waistline, and improves most vegetables, so dab it around—sour cream, too.

Hollandaise is good on every vegetable, too, if your budget allows it.

Grace Rowe's Squash Casserole _____ Serves 6

2 lbs. squash (we
  like to mix yellow
  and zucchini for
  color)
2 carrots, grated
1 onion, chopped
Salt and pepper
1 can cream of
  chicken soup
1 sm. can pimiento,
  chopped and
  drained
1 c. sour cream
8 oz. (2 sticks)
  margarine, melted
8 oz. herb dressing
  mix

Cook squash, carrots and onion together with salt and pepper until tender. Drain and add soup, pimiento and sour cream. Mix melted margarine and herb dressing. Put ¾ of this mixture into squash mixture, and the rest on top. Bake in a baking pan for 30 minutes at 350 degrees.

This is a good dish to freeze uncooked.

Squash Rolls _____ 10 rolls

1¼ lbs. yellow
  squash
½ c. chopped onion
1½ t. salt
½ t. sugar
1 c. cracker crumbs
2 beaten eggs

Cook squash and onion in a little water until tender. Drain and mash. Add remaining ingredients and chill overnight. Then spoon out mixture into 3-inch rolls and roll lightly in cornmeal. Fry in deep fat until firm.

Asparagus in Sauce _____ Serves 6

1½ lbs. fresh
  asparagus (or 2 10
  oz. pkgs. frozen)
1 can mushroom
  pieces
1 can cream of
  mushroom soup
1 c. buttered bread
  crumbs
¼ lb. cheddar
  cheese, grated
¼ c. slivered
  almonds
1 pinch pepper

Cook asparagus in as little water as possible until barely tender. Put in a baking pan. Mix and pour over asparagus the mushroom pieces and cream of mushroom soup. Mix bread crumbs with grated cheese and pour over top. Sprinkle a tiny bit of pepper. Bake in a 350 degree oven for 30 minutes. Serve hot.

Eggs en Cocotte with Asparagus Spears _____ Serves 1

Pour a little melted butter into an individual souffle dish. Add 1 layer of steamed or broiled asparagus spears. Break 1 egg over asparagus without breaking the yolk. Season with salt and pepper. Add ½ eggshell of whipping cream, and butter the size of a hazelnut. Bake in preheated 375 degree oven for 4 or 5 minutes until the egg is done.

(*En cocotte* means in a small earthen cookware)

French Fried Asparagus

Allow 6 asparagus spears per person. Steam asparagus for 6 minutes. Drain and cool to room temperature. Coat each spear with flour, then seasoned and beaten egg yolks and finally bread crumbs. Allow to dry at room temperature for at least 1 hour. Fry a few at a time, in 1 inch of cooking oil, 2 to 3 minutes until each spear is hot and golden brown. Drain on paper towels, and serve at once, piping hot.

Asparagus Casserole

5 potatoes
5 shallots
2 c. asparagus
  (canned, frozen or
  fresh)
¼ c. margarine
Salt and pepper
4 slices cheese

Slice potatoes and put in baking dish, dice shallots and put them on top of potatoes, and put asparagus (cut in 1 inch pieces) on top of that. Asparagus can be arranged to look pretty. Dot with margarine, season, cover tightly and cook at least 45 minutes in the oven, or until potatoes are done. Lay cheese on top and melt before serving.

The amounts are variable and can be changed to fit the amount needed.

Creamed Beets
Serves 6

2 T. vinegar
2 T. butter
Salt and pepper
1 T. water
⅓ c. sour cream
12 small beets,
  cooked, sliced or
  whole

Heat vinegar, butter, salt, pepper and water. When nearly boiling, add sour cream and beets. Continue to heat slowly until beets are hot. Serve at once.

Good Cabbage
Serves 6

1 large head of
  cabbage, chopped
4 T. margarine
4 T. flour
2 c. milk, scalded
1 egg yolk, well
  beaten
1 c. grated cheddar
  cheese
Butter
1 c. cracker crumbs
Pepper and paprika

Cook cabbage; drain. Cook margarine, flour and milk slowly. Add egg yolk, stirring constantly. Season to taste. Add cheese.

In a greased baking pan, place a layer of cabbage and pour cheese sauce over. Dot with butter. Repeat and cover with cracker crumbs, pepper and paprika. Bake in a 350 degree oven until hot.

Sweet Potato Flambée

Serves 6

**6 small sweet
potatoes, boiled**
Salt
4 T. butter
½ c. sugar
½ c. rum

Peel and cut potatoes in half, season with salt, and sauté in the butter in a frying pan until light brown. Remove to a chafing dish or casserole, sprinkle with sugar and pour remaining butter from skillet over. Heat. Just before serving, pour rum on and light.

Hopping John

Serves 6

4 strips bacon
¼ c. chopped onion
**2 c. blackeyed peas,
fresh or frozen**
½ c. raw rice
2 c. water, boiling
Salt and pepper

Dice the bacon and fry with chopped onion. Add the peas, rice and water. Cover and cook at low heat until rice and peas are done. Add seasonings.

This is served in many homes on New Year's Day—for good luck, you know.

Green Beans au Gratin _____ Serves 6

4 T. butter
1 t. salt
4 T. flour
⅛ t. dry mustard
1½ c. milk
½ c. processed cheese, diced or grated
3 c. fresh beans, slivered, cooked in boiling salted water until just underdone
Parmesan cheese
Paprika
Slivered almonds

Melt the butter; add salt, flour and mustard. Cook over low heat until bubbly. Add milk and cook until thick and smooth. Add processed cheese and stir until completely melted. Add beans. Pour into a buttered casserole; sprinkle with Parmesan cheese and paprika. Bake at 350 degrees for 30 minutes, until bubbly. Top with slivered almonds.

Sautéed Fresh Corn _____

Use 2 medium-sized ears for each ½ cup corn. Husk and clean corn, removing the silks carefully. Cut or scrape the kernels from the cob (be sure to get the milk or juice). Place in a skillet with margarine. Cover and cook slowly until the corn is no longer starchy-tasting. Stir frequently. Season with salt and pepper, and if there is any left over after you finish tasting as you go along, serve it hot. Sometimes I add about 2 tablespoon cream for each cup of corn as I sauté it. Allow at least ½ cup of corn per person—it's better to allow a whole cup.

Turnips in Bacon Sauce _____ Serves 6

5 c. turnips, pared
   and diced
3 T. diced bacon,
   fried crisp
½ t. salt
⅛ t. pepper
1 T. flour
1½ t. brown sugar
1 c. condensed milk
2 T. vinegar

Boil turnips in 4 cups water and 1 teaspoon salt for 25 minutes or until tender. Drain. Meanwhile, blend salt, pepper, flour and brown sugar. Then slowly stir in the condensed milk and boil slowly for 2 minutes, stirring constantly. Remove from heat and stir in the vinegar. Add drained turnips and bacon. Serve at once.

Chantilly Potatoes _____ Serves 6

6 large potatoes
2 T. margarine
½ c. milk
Salt and pepper
½ c. whipping
   cream, whipped
   until stiff
4 T. grated American
   cheese
Paprika

Peel and wash potatoes and cook in boiling salted water until done. Drain and mash with margarine and milk and beat until light and fluffy. Season with salt and pepper. Pour into buttered casserole, cover with whipped cream, and sprinkle with cheese and paprika. Bake at 350 degrees until brown on top. Parmesan cheese may be used in place of American.

These are especially good with spicy roast beef.

Party Peas _____ Serves 4

4 strips bacon
¼ c. minced onion
1 T. water
2 T. butter
3 c. frozen peas
   (cooked)
¼ c. shredded lettuce
Salt and pepper
1 t. chopped
   pimiento

Dice bacon and sauté until crisp; remove. Sauté onion in bacon fat until soft; remove and drain. Put water and butter in skillet, add the peas and lettuce, and cook until lettuce is wilted. Add bacon bits and onion; season with salt and pepper. Put pimiento in just before serving.

Broccoli Pudding _____ Serves 6

1 c. medium cream
   sauce
2 well-beaten eggs
   added to cream
   sauce
1 T. lemon juice
1 c. mayonnaise
1½ qts. chopped,
   cooked broccoli

Mix all ingredients together, pour into a buttered 2-quart casserole dish, sprinkle a pinch of nutmeg on top and bake at 325 degrees in a hot water bath until set.

You can cook spinach the same way.

Braised Celery Hearts _____

Use ½ heart per person. Remove leaves and wash thoroughly. Cook until tender in boiling, salted water with an onion and a bay leaf. Remove and cool.

If large hearts are used, split in half. Place in a buttered shallow pan in matchstick formation and cover with a thin brown sauce. I like to use leftover gravy, but you can make a brown sauce with 2 cups bouillon, 2 tablespoons flour and 1 tablespoon butter. Bake at 400 degrees until celery and sauce are thoroughly heated, about 45 minutes.

Celery hearts are now available in cans—and are worth the price. A dish for gourmets!

Despite my book being mainly local mountain foods, I just have to add some of my wonderful recipes given me by some friends from other places. This is my favorite:

————————

Okra Gumbo _____ Serves 12

I start this by making a brown roux first. I always try to have a container of roux in the refrigerator to be able to use on short notice. A roux can be white, blond or brown. They are all made of the same ingredients to begin with, but change in character as heat is applied. All roux consist of flour and fats blended gently over very low heat, from 5 minutes to a much longer period. The roux must be cooked long enough to dispel the taste of raw flour, and long enough to allow the starch and granules to swell evenly, or the sauce will be too thin. White roux should not color, blond barely, and brown should reach the color of hazelnuts to make it smell deliciously baked.

Ingredients for Gumbo:

1 ham hock
3 qts. water
1 whole bunch celery, chopped
4 green peppers, chopped
4 white onions, chopped
4 cloves garlic, chopped fine
2 lbs. sliced okra
1/2 bunch parsley, cut fine
4 T. bacon drippings
4 cans tomatoes
1 can tomato paste
2 T. salt
1 t. freshly ground black pepper
2 T. Lea & Perrins sauce
1 t. hot pepper sauce (or to taste)
1 T. sugar
1 T. paprika
2 lbs. fresh cooked shrimp

Place ham hock in water and let simmer for 30 minutes. Combine next seven ingredients in a skillet and let cook slowly for 30 minutes. Add contents of skillet and remaining ingredients to kettle containing ham hock and water; let simmer for 3 hours. Then add 1 cup roux and stir gently. Let cook about 5 minutes.

De-licious!

This can be a complete meal in itself.

The onion belongs to the lily family—as do chives, ramps, and garlic. It is the most ancient of all cultivated plants. Each has a distinct odor and each has been given a special place in gourmet history.

A good cook will no doubt approach the pearly gates with an onion in one hand and a pound of butter in the other. Onions contain vitamins A and C, and large amounts of minerals, calcium and nitrogen. One medium onion contains 125 calories.

Onions may be added to fritters, to any green vegetable to give a dash, to oyster stew, to sauerkraut, to corn bread, to biscuits, and to pie crusts for meat pies. Our grandmothers had other uses for onions, like onion syrup for colds, and heated or fried onions made in a poultice for croup and earache.

Here are a few things to remember about cooking onions to make them more acceptable:

Red Spanish onion for baking or frying.
White sweet or purple onion for salads.
Yellow onions for stuffing and french frying.
Small white ones for boiling and creaming.
   (Add a dash of vinegar or lemon
   juice to keep them white.)

Broiled Onions on Toast _____

Slice large Bermuda onions paper thin. Put in a long oven-proof casserole. Pour a little olive oil over them and broil to a delicate brown on both sides, turning carefully with a spatula. Place on heavily buttered toast rounds. Sprinkle with Parmesan cheese and run them under the broiler again for a few seconds. Of course use the amount needed for guests.

French-Fried Onions _____

French-fried onions are very popular, too, with steak, or use just as a vegetable, or for a cocktail party. Peel onions, cut in 1/4 inch slices and separate into rings. Dip in milk, drain, and dip in flour. Fry in Crisco (deep) at 370 degrees.

Onion Custard Pie ———————————

I use my favorite pie crust, French Pie Pastry (see index), prebaked. Place an empty pie pan on top of crust to help keep it smooth. Sauté 2 medium onions, that have been chopped coarsely, in butter until yellow and soft. In the meantime, break 5 whole eggs into a bowl. Add 2½ cups milk and mix well together. Add 4 tablespoons flour moistened with a little milk, and season with salt and pepper. Cook this egg mixture quickly in a saucepan, stirring constantly, and add ¾ cup grated cheese and 2 tablespoons Parmesan cheese. Stir until smooth. Season with salt and pepper and a dash of nutmeg. Strain through a colander. Add onions, pour into pie shell and bake at 350 degrees about 30 minutes. Brush with melted butter when finished. Serve hot.

This is good with any kind of beef.

Salads are my favorite foods. But when I think of salads I always think of a horrible experience we had with a fire that burned our kitchen, dining room and 17 guest rooms.

One may call this ESP or just intuition: I had planned to attend the wedding of a dear niece in Norfolk at four o'clock on April 28, 1956. (By the way, this was also the wedding date of the beautiful Grace Kelly to Prince Rainier.) Arrangements were made for me to fly there in the afternoon in time for the wedding. Yet something stronger than my will would not let me go. Ed was too disgusted for words; he packed up his fishing gear and went to the lake.

We were to open for the season the next day. The kitchen had just been completely renovated with new stainless steel tables, tiled floors, and a huge new gas stove. I had just paid the painters for all their work. The delivery trucks from packing houses had just arrived, filling all our new freezers with expensive meats and the extra produce we did not have in our gardens at this time. Everything was in readiness for the guests to arrive the following afternoon—except fresh flowers for the tables.

I had been ill and was forbidden by the doctor to walk. I begged and pleaded with the cook to walk to the pasture with me to gather crab apple blooms to decorate the dining room. She went with me reluctantly—for she knew I should not walk. When we reached the blooms, I looked at my watch and told Margie, the cook, that the wedding was taking place at that moment.

Almost at that instant we heard a terrible explosion. Margie said, "It must be a jet." We turned to look and the dining room was going up in flames! Margie ran to the car, drove to a filling station three miles away and called two fire departments from nearby towns. They came and were able to save some of the guest cottages and our home. It was so hard to watch years of love and hard labor go up on flames. We did not have one penny of insurance.

The North Carolina Highway Patrol went to the lake and found Ed. He was as stunned as I. We were not able to realize for about two days what had really happened. But, as we came out of the shock, I remembered a reservation made by a famous writer for fifty travel editors in three days. John Parris, of the Cherokee Historical Association, was our co-host. Ed said it was out of the question, but I insisted we let them come. I suggested a picnic-style luncheon, but this was out of the question, too, because of the frequent spring showers. But I knew we could not quit.

We borrowed tables and chairs from a nearby school. We ordered from a hotel and restaurant supply house new china, silver, glasses, pots and pans. We revised our menu:

Editor's Menu

Iced Rhubarb Juice—Fresh Fruit Cup—Hot Consommé

A Tray of Stuffed Celery—Radish Roses—Spring Shallots Served with Garlic Toast Points and Cheese Biscuits

Our Own Home Cured Ham Steaks with Minted Green Apples

N.C. Rainbow Trout with Hush Puppies

Little Sugar Peas—New Parsleyed Potatoes

Wilted Lettuce—Special Salad (Branch Lettuce)—Fresh Fruit Salad with Sour Cream or Roquefort Dressing

Spoon Bread—Hot Buttermilk Biscuits

Old Fashioned Vinegar Pie—Strawberry Shortcake—Home Made Ice Cream

Tea—Coffee—Milk

Ed's Chilled Red Grape Wine

We cooked this meal in our family kitchen. We had a large dining area, living room, and we removed the bedroom furniture from two rooms. We served this meal there. I must say it was one of the hardest days of my life, and when two large Trailways buses arrived I had no idea how these out-of-state editors were going to accept this inconvenience. But despite the crowded conditions, this turned out to be the greatest advertisement we ever had.

The salad we served that day was special. It was written up in 17 newspapers, *Holiday, Vogue* and *Redbook*. Needless to say, these write-ups brought us an untold number of guests. They all expected to get this special. Of course, there is a season for "branch lettuce" and only during this time could we serve it. We had people call from two to three hundred miles away to see if we would have the Special Salad.

***

Special Salad (Branch Lettuce)

We picked the lettuce directly from the cold mountain streams. If we were fortunate, we found a ramp to rub the salad bowl with before putting the ingredients in. We chopped the lettuce with young scallions. Then we made a dressing of oil and vinegar with raw eggs beaten in it. We sprinkled the top with croutons that were made in a frying pan, glazing them with butter and garlic.

Be sure the lettuce is as crisp as possible. We crisp it in ice water and when ready to put in a bowl we shake it as dry as possible, then lay it on a turkish towel to get completely dry.

Other salads we like are:

Dandelion Salad

Wash, dry and chill some very young dandelion shoots. These you can find in the fields or even on your lawn. Dice bacon, about 1 slice per serving, and fry crisp; drain and crumble over the greens. Sprinkle with salt and fresh pepper; for enough greens for 4 persons, add ½ teaspoon sugar, ½ tablespoon lemon juice, ½ tablespoon cider vinegar and 3 tablespoons hot bacon drippings, and toss.

Lime Salad Mold   Serves 6

1 3 oz. pkg. lime-
  flavored gelatin
1 c. boiling water
½ c. salad dressing
¼ c. light cream
¾ t. prepared
  horseradish
1 3 oz. can crushed
  pineapple,
  undrained
1 c. cottage cheese
½ c. chopped pecans

Dissolve gelatin in water. Chill until slightly thickened. Blend salad dressing, cream and horseradish. Stir into gelatin. Stir in remaining ingredients. Spoon into mold and chill.

This can also be made with cherry gelatin.

Fruit Salad _____ Serves 4

1 apple, unpeeled,
  chopped
1 orange, peeled and
  sectioned
1/2 c. crushed
  pineapple (drained)
1 pkg. Sweet 'n' Low
3 buds cauliflower,
  grated in blender
1/4 t. coconut extract

Combine, chill, and serve.
Slimming, but delicious.

Boiled Slaw _____ Serves 8

Grate 1 head cabbage and 1 large green pepper and add
1/4 cup sugar. In a saucepan, mix together 1 teaspoon salt,
1/2 teaspoon pepper, 1/2 teaspoon powdered mustard, 1/2
cup of vinegar and 1 cup cooking oil. Let come to a rolling
boil. Pour over cabbage mixture. Put in refrigerator until
ready to use. It will keep, tightly covered, for several days.

Wilted Lettuce _____ Serves 6

We used our own garden oak leaf lettuce. Pick and clean, washing each piece thoroughly. Break (do not cut) into bite size pieces. Slice 6 young scallions over lettuce. Fry 4 to 6 slices of bacon. When the bacon is crisp, take out and drain on a paper towel. Crumble bacon and add to lettuce and onions. Now add 1 teaspoon salt and 2 tablespoons vinegar to the bacon drippings, bring to a boil and pour over the platter of lettuce and onions. Be sure to have some corn bread to eat with it.

Ed's Cheesy Coleslaw Mold _____ Serves 6

1 3 oz. pkg. lime-
    flavored gelatin
1½ c. boiling water
2 T. vinegar
⅓ c. mayonnaise
½ t. salt
Dash pepper
1½ c. shredded green
    cabbage
½ c. shredded carrot
½ c. shredded sharp
    American cheese
⅛ t. celery seed

Dissolve gelatin in boiling water; add vinegar. Combine mayonnaise, salt, pepper; gradually add gelatin mixture. Chill till partially set. Combine chopped cabbage, carrot, cheese and celery seed. Fold into gelatin mixture. Pour into oiled molds. Chill until firm.

Ice Box Salad _____ Serves 8

Break crisp lettuce into a bowl, making a layer. Slice celery thinly and layer on top of lettuce. Briefly boil frozen peas and spread them in a third layer. Sprinkle with a little sugar. Add a layer of minced shallots or onion. Then place a layer of Hellmann's mayonnaise on top. Sprinkle with parmesan. Seal tightly with plastic wrap. Put in refrigerator for several hours.

Rhubarb Salad _____ Serves 8

2 c. chopped raw rhubarb
2 c. pineapple juice
2 pkgs. strawberry gelatin
2 raw apples, diced

Cook rhubarb in pineapple juice until soft. Remove from heat, add gelatin and apples and stir well. Chill until firm.

Beet and Banana Salad _____

Lettuce (Bibb)
1 banana
½ large beet
2 T. sunflower seed
2 T. yogurt

For 1 serving: Make a bed of lettuce on an individual salad plate. Slice banana on top. Slice beet very thinly (but do not grate); add beets on top of banana slices. Sprinkle toasted sunflower seed on top. Then top with yogurt.

This salad is an unusual combination but is colorful and truly delicious.

Spring Dandelion Salad _____ Serves 10

2 qts. tender
    dandelion greens
    (some of the small
    buds are tasty and
    delicious chopped
    in)
1 lb. bacon, fried
    crisp
10 or 12 eggs, beaten
2 T. sugar
1/4 c. vinegar
1/2 t. salt

Wash and chop dandelion greens. Fry bacon and remove to a paper towel and break in small pieces. Pour off grease and pan-fry eggs softly. Add crumbled bacon, sugar, vinegar and salt. Add dandelion greens and just heat through. Vary seasoning to taste. Add a little margarine if you desire.

Spinach Salad _____

Juice of 1 lemon
1 oz. olive oil
1 oz. wine vinegar
Spinach leaves
Tomato, fresh
Chives, fresh
Sugar
Salt and pepper
Bacon, fried and
    chopped

Combine and simmer lemon juice, olive oil and vinegar. Depending on the number of servings, prepare individual salads by placing spinach leaves on a salad plate, then diced tomatoes and chives, lightly sprinkled over. Add sprinkled sugar, salt and pepper and bacon bits. Pour hot lemon juice mixture over salad and serve at once.

BERRYING WE GO

On our many walks through the woods and fields we had seen the snowy white blooms of the strawberry, an occasional blackberry bloom, the frothy white plum flowers, and the blossoms of the wild raspberry, the mulberry, the dewberry, the wild currant, the gooseberry and the wild grape. All of these beautiful blooms seemed enough to ask of nature, but we could not be satisfied with blossoms, for now we were dreaming of our luscious Rum Pot; of delectable strawberry and blackberry jams and jellies, grape conserves and luscious pies; and of Ed's famous wines that he had become an artist at making. It is unbelievable that berries and fruits are free just for the taking. Among our choicest recipes:

Rum Pot

For this pot I used an old glazed stone crock that had a beautiful band of lost blue. This crock was used for many years in my family to make our kraut, pickled beans and chow-chow. In February we had had enough company to use the last morsel of this latter delectable concoction. Therefore, in March, together we managed to haul this precious crock into the sun, where we thoroughly washed it, then left it to air for a couple of days. It got a long rest in April, but come May our crock began long months of work.

We placed the crock in a dry, cool place where it would not be disturbed until the Christmas season.

You can begin your rum pot as we began ours: with a layer of wild strawberries. Carefully hull and clean them, wash them as little as possible, then place them on a cloth to be dried perfectly. Try to bruise as little as possible for this would cause the whole pot to ferment.

Place berries in crock. Sprinkle 1¾ cups sugar over the berries and then pour 1½ quarts of rum down the side of the crock so as not to disturb the berries. You may at first have to weight with a plate until each berry takes enough rum to sink. Be sure the level of the rum is 1¾ inches above the fruit at all times. Cover the pot with plastic and wrap securely. After 4 or 5 days remove the plate and shake gently to help dissolve any remaining sugar. Be sure to keep rum at 1¾ inches above fruit. If any time you go as long as 2 weeks without adding fruit, be sure to shake crock gently and add more rum if necessary.

As soon as cherries are in season, add 1½ pounds of pitted and perfectly cleaned cherries and sprinkle with ¾ pound of sugar. If you are able to get both sweet and sour cherries, add a layer of each. Then add a layer of blackberries in season. Always remember: To 1 pound of fruit add ½ pound of sugar. Next add a layer of currants and a layer of gooseberries (in season). Always keep rum 1¾ inches above fruit. In season add a layer each of black and red raspberries, always remembering sugar and rum. When you add plums, split and stone them. Large pears and peaches may be scalded, peeled, and quartered. Be sure you use a layer of ripe Concord grapes—but seed them first. Pineapple may be added but sure it is fresh and without blemishes. Cut in wedges. Add the last fruit in October.

Seal with plastic wrap and let stand 1 month, undisturbed. Then open the crock and add 2 cups of rum, or enough to bring it 2 inches above top of fruit. Seal again and leave until your Christmas parties. Serve the rum fruit in bowls, plain or with whipped cream. De-licious. A dish you think must have come from above!

While the berries and fruits were in season we scavenged for all the wild ones we could get, but often resorted to our cultivated ones.

Strawberry Preserves _____

Hull and clean 4 cups of ripe strawberries (try to get wild ones). To these 4 cups of berries add 2 cups of sugar and 2 scant tablespoons of vinegar. Let come to a rolling boil. Then add 2 more cups of sugar. Boil gently for 20 minutes. Put in sterilized jars, pour about 1½ tablespoons of paraffin on top of each, and seal.

Blackberry Jam

Wash and clean berries. Put over medium heat to boil. When the berries are cooked soft, run them through a Foley Food Mill. This eliminates most of the seed. For each cup berry pulp, add 1 cup sugar (I never use more than 4 cups of berries at a time). Put over medium heat and boil 20 to 25 minutes. This is wonderful and so easy to make. It cuts out of the jars like jelly. We store it in hot sterilized jars and seal.

Perfect Berry Jam

4 c. berries, packed down (blackberries, strawberries, raspberries—red or black)
4 c. sugar
2 T. margarine
2 T. lemon juice

Combine berries, sugar and butter in a large kettle (not aluminum). Put on stove and cook until butter melts, stirring all the time. Now add lemon juice. Boil and stir for 15 minutes. Let cool a little and stir once in a while. Put in sterilized jars and seal.

This is the very best jam I every tried. It is perfect every time.

Brandied Peaches

4 lbs. sugar
2 c. water
8 lbs. peaches
brandy

Make a syrup of sugar and water; heat to a simmer. Peel peaches and put in cold water to prevent discoloring. Add a few pieces at a time to the syrup and let simmer until tender. Do not let get too soft or they will break. Remove peach slices as they are cooked and place on a cool plate.

Take syrup from fire and add 1 pint brandy to every quart of syrup; stir until cool. Put cooled peaches into sterilized jars, pour syrup over them and seal tightly.

Spiced Blackberries

4 c. brown sugar
2 c. vinegar
5 lbs. blackberries
2 sticks cinnamon
1 T. whole cloves
½ T. whole allspice

Boil sugar and vinegar together for 5 minutes. Add blackberries. Tie spices into a cheesecloth bag and add to blackberry mixture. Let mixture simmer 20 to 25 minutes until it has cooked down thick. Makes about 4 pints.

Aunt Effie's Blackberry Flummery _____ Serves 8

Wash lightly 1 quart of ripe blackberries. Use blender at low speed to thoroughly crush them. Add 1 cup granulated sugar or 1 cup brown sugar. To this add ½ cup cornstarch that is dissolved in just enough water to make a smooth consistency. Cook in a double boiler. Stir constantly to keep from sticking and lumping. Add a pinch of salt. Cook until of the consistency of boiled custard. Chill and served with whipped cream. (Now, we use Cool Whip.)

Mattie's Blackberry Cobbler _____ Serves 4

½ c. **flour**
½ c. **sugar**
½ c. **milk**
1 t. **baking powder**
3 T. **butter**
2 c. **blackberries**

Mix batter of flour, sugar, milk and baking powder. Heat butter in baking pan until melted. Put batter in pan on top of melted butter. Then put berries on top. Bake in a 400 degree oven until brown.

Aunt Effie's Clabbered Squares _____

My Aunt Effie used this as a breakfast dish. It is a most delightful adventure.

Let a pot of sweet milk sour until it can be cut in squares of about ½ inch. Use a berry bowl or small cereal dish to serve this in. Fill ¾ full of clabbered squares and garnish heavily with wild blueberries, raspberries or ripened peaches. Sprinkle lightly with sugar.

One of my aunts used to visit me. She had grown up in the Smokies, but while in college she had married and lived in a large city for many years. After her husband died she came to see me each year, and she loved coming when so many fruits and berries were ripening. She enjoyed making preserves and jellies.

I started out with this woman one day. Her long, narrow face was lined, her hair the color of iron. Suddenly she gave me a queer, rather desperate smile. She said, "This is where Grandpa's barn used to be. We used to have picnics under these trees. I think I remember where these berries grew. When they were ripe they made wonderful pies."

We dawdled near the crumbles of the fieldstone barn. She was in a place she could barely remember since things had changed. Old dirt roads were abandoned, new highways had been built where there had been swamps, and too, my grandfather's land had been requisitioned by the state. The buildings had been torn down and the land was made into a game preserve. Aunt Ess, as we called her, seemed to be lost in painful memory. Suddenly, she went through a clump of hazel trees to discover an ancient roadway that I did not recall existing. I thought I could feel her tremble as she searched for the past. She walked hurriedly as if impatient. Then I saw a laugh in her beautiful grey-green eyes. She had found the remains of the past. There they stood, heavily drooping trees loaded with black mulberries, chokeberries shining red, and entwined fox and fall grapes.

We gathered pailful after pailful. She took a worn white sheet from a basket, spread it under the mulberry trees, and then reached up and gently shook the limbs. We watched the fat, juicy berries plop down.

Aunt Ess said, "Just wait till you taste the pie," and as

we walked back she said, "I think I remember how Ma made it. She used the ripe elderberries to make the same pie." Here is her recipe:

_____

Aunt Ess's Mulberry Pie _____

Line a pie tin with good flaky crust. Fill with ripe mulberries and then sprinkle lemon juice over them. Add 1 cup sugar and a pinch of nutmeg or mace. Cover with a second crust, sealing the edges well by pressing with a fork. Prick top crust a time or two. Bake 35 minutes in a 400 degree oven.

Blackberry Roll _____ Serves 8

This is my mother's recipe and has become a favorite of mine. Sometimes I serve it with afternoon coffee or iced tea, though it is equally good for dessert.

Mix together 2 cups flour, ½ teaspoon salt and 4 teaspoons baking powder. Cut in 4 tablespoons shortening. Lightly mix in 1 cup good grated American cheese and then ⅓ cup milk. Roll dough lightly to ⅓ inch thickness and spread on it 2½ cups blackberries mixed with ½ cup sugar and ¼ cup brown sugar. Roll up like a jelly roll and bake for 45 minutes in a moderate oven until golden brown.

Dampfnudel with Stewed Fruit _____ Serves 8

These dumplings, Aunt Ess remembers, were served with any stewed wild fruits, but especially raspberries. They make a light dessert but my mother always ate them as her noon dinner.

Mix together 2 cups flour, 2 beaten eggs, 1 teaspoon sugar and 1 teaspoon salt. Dissolve ½ envelope or 1½ teaspoons yeast into 1 cup tepid milk; add to flour mixture. Knead the dough and let it rise in a warm place until doubled. Punch down and with floured hands shape lightly into round dumplings. Cover and let rise again in a warm place. When doubled again, drop the dumplings (dampfnudel) carefully into a kettle of salted boiling water or milk; steam them gently for 15 minutes, closely covered, until done. They should be spongy and light and not the least bit moist. Drain them well and carefully, and serve covered with brown butter and a side dish of stewed fresh berries with lots of juice. The berries may be poured right over the buttered dampfnudel if you prefer.

Dewberry Pie _____

When I start thinking of all the delicacies nature has given us, I have no stopping place. Dewberries, or any of the luscious blackberry family, were our favorites for pies. Line a pie pan (9 inch) with pastry and fill it with washed berries. Mix together 1 cup sugar, ¼ cup flour and a dash of salt. Sprinkle this evenly over the berries and dot the top with butter. Adjust the top crust, perforate and bake for 45 minutes in a 400 degree oven. Serve slightly warm with a scoop of ice cream.

Mulberry Jam

This is a surprisingly good jelly with a delicious fruit flavor and a beautiful color. The mulberry doesn't contain enough pectin, however, so it has to be added.

Add ½ cup water to 2 quarts berries and simmer for 5 minutes. Then thoroughly crush the berries and simmer for another 10 minutes. Strain in a cheesecloth bag. To 1 quart strained juice add the juice of 1 lemon and a package of pectin. Bring just to boil again and add 5½ cups sugar. Bring to boil again and boil hard for 1 minute. Skim, pour into jelly glasses and cover with paraffin. Or seal in sterilized ½ pint jars with sterilized lids.

Flower Honey

This recipe, handed down from my Aunt Cora, makes me feel a deep, abiding affection for her memory. It came from her great grandmother Davis.

Pick 6 red clovers, 30 white clovers and 4 full-blown roses. Boil 5 cups sugar with 1½ cups water and 1 level teaspoon alum for a minute, or until clear. Pour over flowers. Let stand 10 minutes and bottle.

It's fun to try on a summer day. Delicious over crêpes.

I had an odd passion for blueberries. They are always found in dry, wild, scrubby fields where we could find enough for winter's hoard of jams, preserves and frozen berries to use in pies. But, oh! how carefully we learned to pick them, for the older people told us the timber rattler liked lying in the sun and part-shade of the blueberry bushes. We always tried to manage to get enough for:

Aunt Ess's Blueberry Cake _____ Serves 6

Beat 1 egg well and stir it vigorously into 5 tablespoons shortening with ½ cup each of white and brown sugar. Sift together 1¾ cups flour, 2 teaspoons baking powder and ¼ teaspoon salt and add to egg mixture alternately with ¾ cup milk, starting and stopping with flour. Toss in ¼ teaspoon grated lemon peel and ½ teaspoon lemon extract; beat well. Lastly, fold in carefully 1 cup fresh blueberries. Bake in 9 inch square pan that is lightly greased, in a 350 degree oven for about 30 minutes. Serve this warm under a slab or dipper of ice cream.

Blueberry Pickle _____

Sterilize glasses and fill with plump, firm blueberries, having first sprinkled them with a little grated lemon rind and ground cloves. Add 1 stick of cinnamon to each jar. Then pour over the berries light molasses, being sure it trickles into all the spaces. Cover only with a cloth, for these will spoil if sealed airtight. Set away and soon the pickle will be sharp and delicious with heavy meats.

Fall Grape Pickles or Preserves _____

My mother used the same method as above, except she filled a 5 gallon crock with the grape mixture. Delicious!

VISITORS
AND FRIENDS

Many years ago we read in the *American* Magazine about a traveling gourmet, Duncan Hines. For some unknown reason—ESP, I guess—I just knew that sometime Duncan Hines would visit us. Often I read about him. As he gained in popularity and renown, I just knew he would come. We had heard that he had a home in Kentucky, so we were intrigued by any Kentucky license plate on a car.

One day four ladies came by for lunch. One carried a small red book. She held it up and said, "We got you out of this book!" Then I saw it was *Adventures in Good Eating* by Duncan Hines. I told them I was sorry but we were not listed—we just wanted to be. Then they turned to the page where we were listed! We still don't understand how we managed to cook the meal for those ladies, our elation was so great. Mr. Hines had written about our country ham, fried apples and hot buttermilk biscuits. This is exactly what the women ordered. We also gave them a watercress salad and freshly made strawberry jam.

This was the beginning of a serious business with us.

Presently we realized that a great part of our clientele was coming from Mr. Hines's recommendations. We had read that he never told you who he was and that if he made a second visit and your food wasn't up to his every standard you would be taken out of his *Adventures in Good*

Eating. We lived in dread that he would come again and find something that was not all right.

Finally, one day he appeared and introduced himself to Ed. I was away shopping. Ed was determined to await my return before he let Mr. and Mrs. Hines eat; fortunately for him there was not even one vacant table. Finally I arrived and Ed met me at the car and very angrily said, "Where have you been? The Duncan Hineses are here and I've stalled as long as possible!"

I went in, bewildered that they had told who they were. Instead of selecting from the menu we had for our outside clientele, he wished to have the regular lunch that our house guests were having (a set menu for boarders). He seemed very pleased with his food and asked for a room for overnight. I was very thankful that we did not have one. However, he had talked to a couple who would be leaving the next morning, and he caught me off guard by asking for this room (which did not have a private bath).

Mr. and Mrs. Hines went to a luxurious hotel in a nearby city for the night. They were back for breakfast the next morning and for the room that was going to be vacant. He had told us already they wanted to spend several days. In a way we felt honored, yet we were afraid he would find something wrong with the food. The following morning they were up early—probably because they had to share a bath.

While breakfast was being prepared, suddenly we were out of water! We called the fire department, and they hauled two truckloads of water, which they poured into the reservoir. The Department of Sanitation worked with us and came and installed a means of disinfecting the water the trucks were putting in.

Many sinister and varied things can happen in the innkeeping business. This time they had really begun to happen to us.

After Mr. Hines had lunch the first day he sat down with us to talk. To get his book up to date, he asked me many questions. Among them was whether we allowed whiskey served in the dining room. My answer was no, for up until this time we had never allowed it. Shortly after this a friendly, playboy type of man from Atlanta came in from his cottage and asked Mr. Hines, "How would you like a mint julep?" Mr. Hines said he would love one. The man ran down to a stream near the house and picked a handful of fresh mint and brought the spirits to go with it. Soon they were having a wonderful time—but in his next printing of *Adventures in Good Eating* Mr. Hines did *not* say we did not allow whiskey in the dining room.

At this time Ed called me aside and told me he thought he should promote a fishing trip, if he could talk the Hineses and many of the guests into going, to give us a chance to catch up on our water. Ed was a great promoter. In two hours he left with 29 guests and some cooks (he took our best one—we did want them to have the very best!)

While Ed and the guests were out fishing, the Jackson County Health Department came to our rescue. They laid a pipeline from our farm pond and pumped water to our reservoir. However, they said we did not have sufficient water to accommodate the number of guests we were catering to.

Ed returned after three days with a tired but happy group of people. To his amazement, we had all the water we could ever use—for I had had a deep well drilled while Ed was away. Necessity makes one do many things that look impossible. This was an expensive adventure but one we were very proud of.

Mr. Hines left not knowing, until two years later on a return trip, that we had been without water and that this was the reason for the glorious fishing outing that was a new experience for him.

Maybe our dinner that night was a very good one, or possibly the Hineses were tired of camp food; at any rate, we had many raves over a stuffed leg of lamb, our own okra casserole, and our fresh rhubarb pie. These, along with other recipes, were included in his next cookbook, and published in syndicated newspapers.

This free advertising helped us to pay for the deep well.

Here are the recipes that were published in *Adventures in Good Eating*:

Stuffed Pork Chops

Use the center cuts of pork chops (as many as you need). Sauté them in butter until slightly brown. Then place on top of each chop, in this order, the following: 1½ tablespoons uncooked rice, a slice of onion, a slice of tomato and a large green pepper ring. Carefully, down the side of the pan, pour enough water to completely cover rice. Cover with a tight cover and place on medium heat (about 300 degrees) until rice is cooked. Serve one chop per person, with a fruit salad and hot rolls.

Julienne Carrots _____ Serves 6

6 good sized carrots
1/2 c. water
1 c. brown sugar
4 T. butter

Cook carrots (with skin on) until tender. Skin and slice in lengthwise strips. Put in baking dish. Combine remaining ingredients in a saucepan and cook until syrupy. Pour over carrots and bake in a 350 degree oven for 20 minutes or until candied.

Corn Pocket Rolls _____ Serves 8

1 1/2 c. flour
1/2 c. cornmeal
2 T. baking powder
1/2 t. salt
2 T. sugar
1 egg, beaten
3/4 c. sour cream
1 T. melted butter

Mix flour, cornmeal, baking powder, salt and sugar. Mix egg and sour cream and combine with dry ingredients. Put on a floured board and roll out rather thin. Brush dough with butter, cut in rounds and fold over. Bake in a 350 degree oven 12 to 15 minutes.

Fresh Rhubarb Pie _____ Serves 8

Clean and cut into 1/2 inch pieces freshly gathered rhubarb. Wash and drain on a cloth. Pour rhubarb into an unbaked pie crust. Mix 1 1/2 cups sugar and 1/2 cup flour. Sprinkle over rhubarb. Then beat 2 eggs and spoon over the flour and sugar. Cut 1/2 stick of margarine over all. Bake in a 350 degree oven until slightly brown and done.

Pie Crust

4 c. sifted flour
1 T. sugar
1½ t. salt
1½ c. shortening
1 egg
½ c. water
1 T. vinegar

Blend flour, sugar and salt. Cut in shortening until flour resembles meal. Beat egg and mix with cold water and vinegar. Sprinkle on flour mixture a tablespoon at a time, tossing with a fork to mix. Gather dough together with fingers until it cleans the bowl. Chill before rolling. This makes two 9 inch crusts.

Fried Apples

Serves 6

Core (peel or not as desired) 6 to 8 Winesap apples. Slice in ½ inch slices like the sections of an orange. Add ½ cup water to apples and cook in covered frying pan until almost tender. Remove the cover and let the water evaporate.

Mix 4 tablespoons bacon drippings and ⅔ cup sugar. Add to apples and fry until apples are a deep golden brown and candied. Turn frequently while browning.

Stuffed Leg of Lamb _____ Serves 10

From a 6 pound leg of lamb, have butcher remove H
bone and center bone, leaving the shank bone forming a
pocket where bones have been removed. Thinly slice 2
slices bacon and 6 chicken livers. Cook together until
slightly browned. Remove and reserve. In bacon drippings
cook 1 sliced onion and 1 chopped clove garlic over medium heat until soft; drain fat. Break 4 cups soft bread
crumbs and mix with onion, garlic, bacon and livers. Add 1
teaspoon oregano, 1 tablespoon minced parsley, ¾ teaspoon salt and ¼ teaspoon black pepper. Mix all well. Put
stuffing in pocket and on flattened bone end. Tie roast
with clean white cord. Rub roast with softened butter or
oil. Sprinkle with 1½ teaspoons salt, ½ teaspoon rosemary
or oregano and 1½ tablespoons lemon juice. Roast 1½
hours in a 400 degree oven for rare meat or 1¾ hours for
medium rare.

Always in the innkeeping business there was a "help"
problem. This was the reason it was essential to know how
to be proprietor, cook, dishwasher and all-purpose maid.

With the beginning of World War II, many people left
our beautiful countryside seeking employment in defense
jobs in large cities. We had no idea where we could seek
help.

Always, it seemed, something would turn up if you
lived right—or that was how we had found it. It was at this
time we were visited by a Catholic priest, who told us his
church was sponsoring some prisoners of war from Europe
and we could get one to work for us for an indefinite
period of time. We were told to pay this person $1.00 per

week. We accepted his proposition. We were to be notified on the arrival of the person. We were to take either male or female.

Soon we were called to come to a motel in Waynesville to pick up our POW. We were surprised that instead of one there were two, a Polish man and his wife. We were elated! To us they were John and Mary—we were given no other name. They could not speak one word of English.

I shall never forget those sad, sad faces. At first, we had the feeling they did not trust us. When we arose early in the morning, they were waiting for us. They were very willing to work, but it was a problem communicating. They could only do what they saw to do. Mary was so trustworthy and learned to understand some things from me very fast. John always seemed willing to try if we were able to make him understand.

Soon Mary became my right hand as a kitchen helper. But we could not let them do this work without receiving the right pay—the same as we paid our other workers. Every night we could hear them counting their money. Besides their salaries from us, they received good tips from the guests.

Once a week a priest visited them. John was soon able to convey to us that they were required to give part of their money each week to the priest. He was angry to have to divide their earnings. Sweet Mary never showed any regrets. Each day we learned to depend on them and they on us.

Always there were amusing incidents happening. One day it was the day for the cook to be off. I was depending on Mary to help me prepare dinner for 75 guests. I thought she understood we would begin at three o'clock. When the time came there was no Mary. Four and five o'clock came and still we could not find her. John could not understand that we were worried. He did all he could in the kitchen, but he was little help. Finally Ed and I got the dinner ready, after which Ed tried to make John understand we must find Mary.

Presently she showed up. She was filthy from the top of her head to her toes. John laughed and laughed, then went to their room for clean clothes while she went to an outside shower. Then John took Ed by the hand and took him to our pig pens, where we had nine fattening hogs. There they found that Mary had been washing the pens and the hogs. Every hog had been washed with soap and water. Ed said they were almost a beautiful pink and the pens were spotless. They made us understand this had to be done once a week if we intended to kill them for meat. This was the Polish way. Ours were the cleanest pigs in the whole countryside.

Soon Mary was making the most delectable Polish dishes. Among some of her recipes that were our favorites are:

Mary's Sweet Rolls (Brioche)

1 c. milk
½ c. margarine
1 t. salt
½ c. sugar
2 yeast cakes or 2 T.
  dry yeast
¼ c. lukewarm water
4 beaten eggs
1 t. grated lemon
  rind
4½ c. sifted flour
Melted butter

Scald milk in upper part of a double boiler; stir in the margarine, salt and sugar. Cool until lukewarm. Dissolve yeast in the lukewarm water and add eggs and lemon rind. Add to milk mixture. Add flour; beat well. Cover lightly with a cloth and let rise in a warm place, not hot, until doubled in bulk, about 3 hours.

Knead and cut off one-quarter of the dough for "head" of brioches. Rub muffin pans with shortening. Shape dough from larger portion into balls that half-fill the muffin tins. Then with your thumb make an indentation on each ball and brush with melted butter. From the one-quarter of the dough, make small pear-shaped balls. One small ball of dough, pointed side down, should be pressed into the indentation in each of the larger balls. Brush with melted butter. Let pans stand uncovered in a warm place about 30 minutes. Bake in a 425 degree oven for about 20 minutes. Remove at once from the pans. Makes approximately 36 2-inch brioches. Delicious when split and toasted, even after a week old. Sometimes Mary would put jam or jelly in the indentations before cooking.

Beef Rollups (Polish)

2 lbs. round steak cut
  1/4 in. thick
2 t. salt
1/2 t. pepper
2 c. soft bread
  crumbs
1 sm. minced onion
1 egg, slightly beaten
1/2 c. margarine,
  divided and melted
Flour
2 c. water or meat
  stock
1 T. chopped parsley

Cut round steak into strips about 4 1/4 by 2 inches. Sprinkle with part of salt and pepper. Pound with a wooden mallet or the edge of a plate to flatten pieces. Combine bread crumbs, onion, egg, 1/4 cup of the melted margarine and remaining salt and pepper. Spread mixture on pieces of meat, roll up and fasten with toothpicks. Dredge rollups with flour and brown in remaining 1/4 cup margarine. Add water or meat stock. Cover and simmer for 2 hours, or until meat is tender. Remove toothpicks and place rollups on heated platters. Pour the gravy over the rollups; sprinkle with chopped parsley. Serve with mashed potatoes.

Despite our differences, we learned to love John and Mary, and I believe the feeling was mutual.

One day a priest drove up in a truck. Both Mary and John went out to the truck. They talked to some extent, sometimes loudly and with emotion. Then the three of them went to Mary and John's room and soon we saw them loading their bundles, tied in blankets they had brought with them. Both John and Mary came to us, kissing our hands, with tears streaming down their cheeks. When Ed asked the priest what was taking place, the priest's answer was, as he shrugged his shoulders, "It is time for them to go."

The relationship between our Polish employees and ourselves was the best. They were happy here and went away with money, as far as we knew. We never saw or heard from them again. All we could say was, our association with these Polish people made us think all Polish people are the finest among God's chosen few.

———————

After our first season, we did a little advertising. At this time people were looking for family-type places to stay for the summer. Therefore, at once, we began establishing a wonderful and stable clientele.

Among our most valued and well-liked guests were a former actress and her husband, a Frenchman and a former hotel man. They loved the countryside and, fortunately, they liked us. They spent three full years with us, teaching and guiding us in what turned out to be a big adventure for us.

He taught us every phase of catering to the traveling public—from writing letters to prospective guests to bidding them adieu. He made us very food-conscious. They took us many places, and we learned a great deal about how other people do things. They taught us what crêpes suzettes were and how to make and serve them. They taught us unusual hors d'oeuvres. With them we had our first pheasant under glass and crème brulée and caviar omelette.

These experiences were an important education for us, teaching us things we needed to know as our clientele grew. For no matter how modest an eating place or inn, you will find yourself catering to celebrities of every sort. We catered to the cotton mill hands and factory workers.

We entertained VIPs from the political world. We had members of the United States president's cabinet; many governors from many states, judges, bishops, clergymen and famous evangelists, TV personalities and one very, very famous actress were among our guests. Admirals, generals and all high officials from the armed services from both the United States and England visited us. We had counts and countesses from other lands and thousands of everyday, wonderful people who made life worth living.

We entertained the Walt Disney Company for three weeks. Our experiences with them were many and varied, some happy, others not so happy. Believe me, it is a task to make and pack $4,000 worth of box lunches over a period of three weeks. I'd never want to tackle a job like that again. But I will give you some of the most popular sandwiches with this group of 120 people:

Barbecued Hamburger for a Crowd _____ Serves 8

4 lbs. ground beef
5 green peppers,
  chopped
5 onions, chopped
2 c. celery, chopped
2 12oz. bottles catsup
1 c. brown sugar
1 c. mustard
$^{1}/_{2}$ c. Worcestershire
  sauce
$2^{1}/_{2}$ t. chili powder
Salt and pepper to
  taste

Brown beef, green peppers, onions and celery; add remaining ingredients. Cook gently for 2 hours. Serve on split buns. (This was most popular.)

Ham Custard Sandwiches —————————— Serves 8

16 slices of bread,
   crust removed
Butter, softened
2 c. ground ham
2 t. mustard
¼ t. garlic salt
1 c. sharp grated
   cheese
2-3 eggs
2 c. milk

Butter bread on both sides. Arrange 8 slices in a large pan. Place ham mixed with mustard and garlic salt on bread. Sprinkle cheese over all. Place remaining 8 slices of bread on top. Mix eggs and milk and pour over all. Let stand 1 hour or longer. Cover with foil. Cook at 350 degrees for 1 hour or until brown.

Reuben Sandwich —————————— Serves 10 - 12

3 lbs. corned beef
1 one lb. 11 oz. can
   of chopped kraut
20 to 24 slices rye
   bread with caraway
   seed
Butter
1 lb. sliced imported
   Swiss cheese

Place the corned beef in a deep kettle or casserole and cover with cold water. Bring to a boil, cover and simmer gently for 50 minutes per pound, or until tender. Thirty minutes before cooking is scheduled to be finished, pile sauerkraut on top of meat.

When cooking is finished, slice corned beef and drain the sauerkraut.

For each sandwich, toast two slices of rye bread. Butter each slice on one side. Place one piece buttered side up; top with several slices of hot corned beef and drained sauerkraut over corned beef. Arrange slices of Swiss cheese over sauerkraut and broil until cheese melts. Top with remaining piece of toast, buttered side down.

As I have said earlier, our guests were many and varied. Sometimes we would stop and wonder who would come next.

One rainy afternoon an old foreign car drove up. A man and a woman appeared. We had heard the word beatnik and this is what we saw! That was how the man looked, but the woman was the most beautiful creature we had yet seen. In broken English they told us they wished to stay for the night. The next day they asked to stay for a few days, saying they liked the place, the food, and the countryside.

Each day they would go walking. Soon we learned he was a Polish count; she, his countess, was born in Switzerland but had lived in Poland for several years. In a very few days we were to learn both were world famous—she a sculptress and he an archeologist.

It was through the count that we gained much publicity and a few days of an anticipation that is hard to describe.

Late one evening, after one of his daily walks, the count told Ed he had made an amazing discovery. He had found what he believed to be an ancient buried village, and he wanted permission to unearth it.

It was agreeable to us as it was on a pasture hill that would not interfere with our business.

With the help of a couple of laborers, he began digging in the hill. As the men worked, the count paid a visit to the Asheville *Citizen* promoting his project.

The *Citizen* did some beautiful stories and pictures of the "Hidden or Buried Village." Many people came looking. Finally the count said we would have to have a two-way road to our place. The state transportation board sent engineers to lay out a road and to build it. In the meantime, it was found out that this was a promotion deal to get money to finish his excavation. He dug long enough to find huge layers of rock that looked as if they had been placed there; he also found a few pieces of pottery.

One day he told Ed he had to go to New York to get money to further his work. He also asked if he should hire guards or watchmen to see that no one bothered the hill. My brother was there and told him, "Hell, people around here are too lazy to dig their potatoes; they'd never tackle those huge stones." He left. We never saw or heard of them again except in newspapers and magazines.

As I related earlier, the countess was a sculptress. She evidently believed her body a beautiful one for always in her room she was nude. It made no difference if she had asked for a maid or a man to lay a fire in her fireplace, she never bothered to put on a robe.

On their long walks she found many edible mushrooms. She would gather them and bring them home to be cooked. She taught us to "tell" the edible ones and taught us to cook many recipes. Here are some:

Raw Mushroom Salad _____ Serves 6

She used the meadow mushrooms, the puff balls and the little club-shaped corals. Any of these are delicious in a salad. You will need 1 pound of mushrooms, 1 large celery heart and 4 hard boiled eggs. Don't chop any of these but cut them in bite-size pieces. Rub a deep salad bowl with a cut clove of garlic, then put the above ingredients in it. Add 1 finely minced sweet red pepper and 2 minced shallots or scallions on top. Season to taste with salt and pepper and toss in a dressing made of 4 parts cold-pressed olive oil to 1 part wine vinegar. Toss for several minutes, then set in the refrigerator for about 1 hour to ripen and blend. Serve on lettuce leaves.

Stuffed Mushrooms _____ Serves 8

Meadow mushrooms are good stuffed. The best stuffing mushrooms of them all is the morel. Sauté 8 to 10 large morel caps in margarine until about half done, then remove and keep them warm. Next, sauté 1 finely minced onion, and the stems and any rejected caps of the morels. When they look done, add 1/4 pound ground beef, 1 teaspoon salt, and a dash of monosodium glutamate. Let this cook for only a minute, then turn the heat off and add 1/2 cup cooking sherry. Now stir in enough dry bread crumbs to make a fluffy mixture and carefully stuff the morel caps without breaking them apart. Set them in a casserole and bake for 30 minutes in a 350 degree oven. Serve hot.

Mushroom Fritters _____ Serves 6

Sauté 1 pound of mushrooms, drain and save juice. Chop mushrooms fine. Let the juice cool, then mix it with 2 beaten eggs. Sift together 1½ cup flour, 2 teaspoons baking powder, 1 teaspoon monosodium glutamate, ½ teaspoon salt and a little freshly ground pepper. Add the egg-juice mixture and the chopped mushrooms and mix well. Drop by spoonfuls in shallow cooking oil heated to 375 degrees. Fry until nicely browned; this will take about 3 minutes. Drain on paper towels. Serve piping hot.

Among our clientele were regular tour groups from New York City; Washington, D.C.; Cleveland, Ohio; and Des Moines, Iowa. There were usually 50 persons on each bus. The tourists ranged in age from the very young to the very old. Their guides were always accomplished in their occupations. Usually these guides were young men in or just out of college. Such a joyful group usually came. The "Corn Huskers" from Iowa always seemed particularly congenial with our people and with each other.

The guides had always given us such a build-up that we were on the alert to please our guests, and I can truthfully say I don't believe we ever had a disappointed guest among them.

We always had a set menu. We had Mountain Trout with Hush Puppies, Stuffed Cornish Hens, Fried Chicken or our own Sunset Farms Broiled Country Ham Steak. The guide made a list of what his group wished for the next day's lunch; then he would call me from the hotel in Asheville where they were staying, giving me their wishes. Therefore, we were ready for them when they arrived. After the meals were served, they usually wanted to walk over the grounds—to see any vacant rooms we might have.

This was good advertisement. Many returned for their vacation or sent others.

It is a strange thing that these tour people seemed to be intrigued by the names of our desserts. They either wanted Vinegar Pie or Sauerkraut Cake. Maybe the tour guides played them up. Here are the recipes:

Vinegar Pie _____ Makes two 10 inch pies

3 sticks margarine
3¾ c. sugar
9 eggs
6 T. vinegar
9 T. milk
3 t. flour
3 t. vanilla

Melt margarine. Add sugar, then add beaten eggs, vinegar, milk, flour and vanilla. Pour into 2 uncooked 10 inch pie shells and bake at 350 degrees in preheated oven until done.

Sauerkraut Cake _____ Serves 40

5 c. sugar
2½ c. shortening
1½ t. salt
1¾ c. cocoa
11 eggs
4½ c. all purpose
  flour (sifted 4
  times)
1½ T. baking powder
1½ T. soda
1 qt. water
2 c. well-drained
  chopped kraut
Icing (see below)

Mix the ingredients as given in order, creaming as usual in all cakes. Bake 45 minutes in a 350 degree oven. Spread icing over cooled cake.

Icing _____

2 c. sugar
½ c. milk
½ c. cocoa
½ c. butter
1 t. vanilla

Mix all ingredients, bring to boil and boil for 1 minute. Beat briskly until it is of spreading consistency.

Some of the more popular cake recipes that were given me by friends, my mother and other relatives, are:

Joyce's Easy Does It Fruit Cake _____ Serves 25

1 lb. candied cherries
1 lb. candied
  pineapple
1 lb. chopped dates
1 lb. shredded
  coconut
2 c. English walnuts
3 c. pecans
4 c. sweetened Eagle
  Brand Condensed
  Milk

Mix all ingredients in order given. Put in a well-greased tube cake pan, bake in a 250 degree oven for 3 hours. Excellent!

Grace's Italian Cream Cake _____ Serves 15

1 stick margarine
½ c. Crisco
2 c. sugar
5 egg yolks
2 c. flour
1 t. soda
1 c. buttermilk
1 t. vanilla
1 sm. can angel flake
  coconut
1 c. chopped pecans,
  plus extra for
  garnish
5 stiffly beaten egg
  whites
Cream Cheese
  Frosting (see
  below)

Cream margarine and Crisco; add sugar and beat until mixture is smooth. Add egg yolks and beat well. Combine flour and soda and add to creamed mixture alternately with buttermilk. Stir in vanilla. Add coconut and pecans. Fold in stiffly beaten egg whites. Pour batter in three greased 8 inch pans. Bake at 350 degrees for 25 minutes. Frost with Cream Cheese Frosting. Garnish with extra chopped pecans.

Cream Cheese Frosting _____

1 8 oz. pkg. cream
  cheese, softened
½ stick margarine
1 box powdered
  sugar
1 t. vanilla

Beat cream cheese and margarine until smooth; add sugar and mix well. Add vanilla and beat until smooth. Spread between layers and on top and sides of cake. Frosts three 8 inch layers.

Sara Jean's Brown Sugar Pound Cake _____ Serves 12

2 sticks butter
$\frac{1}{2}$ c. Crisco
1 box plus 1 c. light
  brown sugar
5 eggs
$3\frac{1}{2}$ c. flour, sifted
  before measuring
$\frac{1}{2}$ t. baking powder
1 c. sweet milk
$1\frac{1}{4}$ t. vanilla

Cream butter and Crisco until fluffy. Add sugar, one cup at a time, and cream thoroughly. Add eggs one at a time, blending thoroughly after each addition. Sift flour again with baking powder. Add these dry ingredients alternately with milk to the creamed mixture. When thoroughly mixed add vanilla. Pour into a well greased and floured tube pan. Bake at 325 degrees for $1\frac{1}{2}$ hours.

Eddie's Old Fashioned Cream Cake—Never Fails ___ Serves 12

2 sticks margarine
3 c. sugar
6 eggs
1 c. whipping cream
$\frac{1}{2}$ t. baking powder
3 c. cake flour
1 t. vanilla
1 t. lemon extract

Cream margarine until fluffy. Add sugar a little at a time, beating, until mixture is fluffy. Add eggs one at a time, beating after each addition. Sift cake flour with baking powder. Add whipping cream and cake flour alternately to creamed mixture, beginning and ending with flour. Add vanilla and lemon. Pour batter into a greased and floured tube pan. Bake $1\frac{1}{2}$ hours in a 300 degree oven.

Louise's Upsadaisy Cake _____ Serves 12

For the upside down frosting:
- 5 T. butter
- 2 T. cream
- ¾ c. brown sugar (firmly packed)
- ¾ c. coconut
- ¾ c. chopped California walnuts

For the cake:
- 3 eggs
- 1 t. vanilla
- ½ t. lemon extract
- 1½ c. sugar
- 1½ c. cake flour
- 1½ t. baking powder
- ½ t. salt
- ¾ c. milk
- 1½ T. butter

Prepare the frosting first: In a saucepan heat the butter and cream, stir in the brown sugar, coconut and nuts, and cook gently, stirring, until well blended. Spread evenly over the bottom of a large (8 x 12) baking pan, and set aside while you make the cake.

Put eggs, vanilla and lemon extract into a mixing bowl; beat with rotary beater, adding sugar gradually, and continue beating until fluffy. Sift flour, baking powder and salt together, add to egg mixture and beat thoroughly. Heat milk and butter together just to the boiling point, add gradually to batter and beat slightly. Pour batter over prepared frosting in pan, and bake in a moderate oven, 350 degrees, for 35 minutes. When done, loosen edges and turn out upside-down on a rack to cool. Any frosting sticking to the pan may be scraped out while hot and spread on the cake.

Cold Oven Pound Cake _____ Serves 15

3 c. sugar
1/2 c. butter or
   margarine
1/2 c. Crisco
5 large eggs, or 6
   medium
3 c. flour
1 c. milk
1 t. vanilla
1 t. lemon
1/2 t. baking powder

Have all ingredients at room temperature. Cream sugar, butter and Crisco until fluffy. Add eggs one at a time, beating after each addition. You may use electric mixer or your hands. Blend in flour and milk alternately, starting and ending with flour. Add flavorings, mix well.

Sprinkle the 1/2 teaspoon baking powder on top and mix, but not too hard. Then beat at medium speed with mixer for 10 minutes.

Lightly grease a tube pan and line the bottom with waxed paper. Pour batter into pan. Put in a cold oven. Set at 350 degrees and bake for 1 hour and 15 minutes.

Lemon Cake Pudding _____ Serves 20 - 25

Sift together 3/4 cup flour, 3 cups sugar, and 3/4 teaspoon salt. Stir in 4 1/2 teaspoons grated lemon rind and juice, 6 beaten egg yolks and 3 cups milk. Fold in 6 stiffly beaten egg whites. Pour into a 9 x 16 pan. Set this pan in a pan of water 1 inch deep. Bake at 350 degrees for 45 to 50 minutes.

Cranberry Cake _____ Serves 12

2¼ c. flour
1 c. sugar
¼ t. salt
1 t. baking powder
1 t. soda
1 c. chopped pecans
1 c. diced dates
1 c. whole
  cranberries
Grated rind of 2
  oranges
2 eggs, slightly
  beaten
1 c. buttermilk
¾ c. salad oil
1 c. confectioners'
  sugar (10x)
1 c. orange juice

Sift together flour, sugar, salt, baking powder and soda. Stir in nuts, dates, cranberries and orange rind. Combine eggs, buttermilk and salad oil. Add to flour and fruit mixture and stir until blended. Pour in a well greased tube pan and bake for 1 hour at 350 degrees. Remove to plate placed over wide pan. Mix superfine sugar and orange juice; spoon over warm cake until absorbed. Wrap in foil 24 hours before serving.

This is moist and luscious.

Scottish Shortbread _____ Serves 20

1 lb. butter
1 c. fine sugar
4 c. flour

Mix to a dough using your hands. Press and pat into a cookie sheet. Prick with a fork in a pattern or just helter-skelter. Bake 10 minutes at 400 degrees, then turn the oven back to 325 degrees and bake for 25 minutes. Cut in squares while hot. Do not remove from the sheet until cold. Store in cookie jar.

I used them for afternoon tea.

The Perfect Chocolate Cake _____ Serves 10 - 12

For the cake:
  1 c. unsifted
    unsweetened
    cocoa
  2 c. boiling water
  2¾ c. sifted all-
    purpose flour
  2 t. baking soda
  ½ t. salt
  ½ t. baking
    powder
  1 c. margarine,
    softened
  2½ c. granulated
    sugar
  4 eggs
  1½ t. vanilla
    extract

Make cake: In a medium bowl, combine cocoa with boiling water, mixing with wire whisk until smooth. Let cool completely.

Sift flour with soda, salt and baking powder. Preheat oven to 350 degrees. Grease well and lightly flour three 9 x 1½ inch layer cake pans.

In large bowl of electric mixer, at high speed, beat margarine, granulated sugar, eggs and vanilla, scraping bowl occasionally with rubber scraper, until light, about 5 minutes. At low speed, beat in flour mixture (in fourths), alternately with cocoa mixture (in thirds), beginning and ending with flour mixture. Do not overbeat. Divide evenly into prepared pans; smooth tops. Bake 25 to 30 minutes or until surface springs back when gently touched with fingertips. Cool in pans 10 minutes. Carefully loosen sides with spatula; remove from pans; cool on wire racks.

For the frosting:
  1 pkg. (6 oz.)
    semisweet
    chocolate pieces
  ½ c. light cream
  1 c. margarine
  2½ c. unsifted
    powdered sugar

Make frosting: In medium saucepan combine chocolate pieces, cream and margarine; stir over medium heat until smooth. Remove from heat. With wire whisk, blend in powdered sugar in a bowl set over ice; beat until it holds shape.

For the filling:
- 1 c. heavy cream, chilled
- ¼ c. unsifted powdered sugar
- 1 t. vanilla extract

Make filling: Whip cream with powdered sugar and vanilla; refrigerate.

Place cake on a serving plate, top side down; spread with ½ the filling. Place second layer top side down; spread remaining filling. Place third layer top side up, on top.

With spatula, frost sides of cake first, covering whipped cream; use remaining frosting on top, swirling decoratively. Refrigerate at least 1 hour before serving.

To cut, use a sharp, thin-bladed knife; slice with sawing motion.

Mandarin Orange Cake   Serves 10

For the cake:
- 2 c. sugar
- 2 c. plain flour
- 2 t. soda
- ½ t. salt
- 2 eggs, well beaten
- 2 cans mandarin oranges, well drained

Sift all dry ingredients together. Add oranges to eggs and beat on low speed until oranges are all to pieces. Add dry ingredients and then pour in a well greased and floured 9 x 13 pan. Bake at 350 degrees for 30 minutes in preheated oven.

For the topping:
- ¾ c. packed light brown sugar
- 3 T. milk
- 2 T. butter

Mix ingredients and bring to a boil. Spoon over hot cake as it is brought from oven. When cool, serve with Cool Whip.

Cornmeal Sour Cream Pound Cake _____ Serves 16

1 c. margarine
2 c. sugar
1 t. vanilla
Pinch of salt
6 egg yolks
1½ c. plain flour
1½ c. plain cornmeal
¼ t. soda
1 c. sour cream
6 egg whites
¼ t. salt

Grease and flour tube pan. Cream margarine and sugar until real creamy. Add vanilla and pinch of salt. Add egg yolks, one at a time, beating well after each. Sift flour, cornmeal and soda together three times. Add alternately with sour cream to the above creamed mixture. Add salt to egg whites and beat until peaks form. Fold egg whites into the mixture. Pour into pan and bake 1 hour at 350 degrees.

AUTUMN

The autumn is the season we loved. We loved the beautiful colors of leaves, the blue, blue skies, the crispy mornings, and knowing that frost was in the air. We knew, too, that there was work to be done. We had to harvest and save for the long, snowy winter days. The lovely Indian summer days were to be enjoyed, and along with harvest chores there were so many varied works and pleasures.

We hauled in load after load of wood to enjoy in the fireplace. Also in wood-burning season, we loved baking cracklin' bread in the coals of the wood oven. It took only a few coals under the oven and a few for the top. One must keep watching and turning it to prevent scorching, and it needs to cook slowly. Have plenty of milk in the refrigerator to drink with it. Also, we think this is a good time to boil a pot of leather britches—cooked at the open fire in an iron pot with a rasher of salt pork.

Here is my cracklin' bread my mother taught me to make:

———————————

Cracklin' Bread _____ Serves 6

3 c. cornmeal
2 t. salt
½ c. flour
3 t. baking powder
1 egg, beaten
2½ c. sour milk
2½ c. cracklings

Mix all dry ingredients. Mix well with egg and milk and add cracklings. Bake in a greased hot pan in hot oven for 25 to 30 minutes.

Leather Britches _____

We string the beans and dry them in the hulls until they are perfectly dry and put them away in a dry place. When it comes time to cook them, we take them out the night before and let them soak overnight in water. Then we wash them again and cover with water in which we have put several rashers of fatback or salt pork and boil slowly until the bean is soft when mashed between your fingers. We, of course, salt the beans—use about 1½ tablespoons salt.

In late September the apples glowed on the trees and were sweetening for gathering time. Also, as we looked across the wide fields of drying corn we saw an occasional large yellow pumpkin.

September was an in-between time. The toil was almost over. We were waiting for the ripeness of the harvest. There was a strange restlessness rooted deep in the past when man and animal feared hunger, cold and all the uncertainties that come with winter. We watched and waited for the right time and always saved and stored more than we could use.

This is the time we searched the gardens for the last of tomatoes, cabbages, peppers and corn that we utilized for the most delicious chow-chow. We will give our recipe later in this chapter.

Just before the danger of an early frost, the turnips, carrots and late cabbage were taken to the root cellar, or sometimes we stored them in the garden itself under an insulation of corn stalks, straw or grass, and about two feet of earth; there they would keep and sweeten for late winter and spring use.

But before the cabbages were stored, large baskets of them were trimmed, washed and finely chopped for the kraut crock, or sometimes later on we used Mason jars to pack it in. In each case the containers were carried to the cellar where, in course of time, nature's chemistry worked the change that makes these sweet, delicious, crisp cabbages into a sour delicacy.

Kraut

We use a large wooden bread tray to chop cabbage in (we like it chopped rather than shredded). Then we fill the crock into which we have put 1 tablespoon salt to each gallon of cabbage. We weight the cabbage down with a plate and a heavy, clean rock on top. We then let it stand, lightly covered with a cloth, until kraut is made.

Kraut in Mason jars is our favorite. Chop as you do above. Pack in 1 quart Mason jars that have been thoroughly sterilized. Add 1 teaspoon salt to top of jar. Pour boiling water over, then cover with a washed, clean grape leaf. Seal jars as tightly as possible. Store in a dark place. When it begins to ferment, the seal will be broken, but don't disturb—it will reseal when kraut is made.

Pickled Beans

Prepare beans as for table. Cook until just tender (not soft), then wash and drain. Fill jars but do not pack (I use quart Mason jars with rubbers and old fashioned lead lids).

Make a solution of $\frac{1}{2}$ cup salt, 1 cup vinegar and 1 gallon warm water. Mix and dissolve well. Pour over beans that are in the jars until water overflows. Put jars in a cool, dark place. Be sure to tighten lids. Seal will be broken when beans are working but will reseal when beans are pickled.

Homemade Hominy _____ 10 Servings

Shell one quart of corn and place in cooking pot (a black iron one is best). Boil for 1 hour. In a white flour sack tie one quart of clean wood ashes from stove; add this bag to pot of corn. Cook slowly all day. Wash and drain corn in cold water. The hulls will come off and come to top where you can remove them. Stew washed, drained corn in bacon drippings or butter. Good!

Pickled Okra _____

Garlic (1 clove for each jar)
Hot pepper (1 for each jar)
Okra, washed young tender pods
Dill seed (1 t. for each jar)
1 qt. white vinegar
1 c. water
½ c. salt

Place the garlic and hot pepper in the bottom of clean, hot, sterilized pint jars. Pack firmly with clean, young okra from which the stems have been removed. Stem end must be open. Add dill seed. After packing jars, bring vinegar, water and salt to a boil. Simmer about 5 minutes and pour while boiling hot over okra. Seal immediately. The above pickling solution will fill from 5 to 7 pint jars.

Chow-Chow

1 doz. medium
  onions
1 doz. sweet green
  peppers
1 doz. sweet red
  peppers
4 qts. chopped
  cabbage
2 qts. chopped green
  tomatoes
$\frac{1}{2}$ c. salt
5 c. sugar
4 T. mustard seed
4 T. ground mustard
1 T. turmeric
1 T. ground ginger
3 t. celery seed
2 T. whole mixed
  pickling spice (tied
  in a bag)
$2\frac{1}{2}$ qts. vinegar

Chop onions and peppers fine. Combine all vegetables and mix with salt. Let stand overnight. The next morning drain well. Combine sugar, spices and vinegar. Bring to a boiling point and simmer for about 20 minutes. Add drained vegetables, and simmer to consistency desired. Remove spice bag. Pack hot chow-chow into sterilized jars and seal.

We eat with dried beans or any legumes.

Johnnie Ruth's Malt Sweet Pickle Chips _____

Take 1 gallon of cider vinegar; dissolve 2 cups of pickling salt in it (cold).

Put whole, clean cucumbers in a jar or crock; pour the above mixture over them and let stand 10-12 days.

Pour off brine, drain well, rinse crock. Slice cucumbers (measure as you go) and put them back into the crock. Add ½ as much sugar as you have cucumbers. Add 5 tablespoons *malt* vinegar.

Let stand 2 - 3 days, stirring often. Ready to eat!

If you have more cucumbers, adjust your amounts. Have enough brine to cover. I weight mine down with a plate and a large rock so as to keep them in the brine.

They will keep in the crock, or I put them in glass jars and put lids on them. But *do not heat*.

Stuffed Hot Banana Peppers, Pickled _____

Chop cabbage as for slaw. Pour boiling water into peppers that have had seeds removed. Let sit for 15 minutes. Then empty water completely out of each pepper. Stuff peppers with finely chopped cabbage. Boil 3 quarts water with 1 quart white vinegar; add ½ cup salt and 1 teaspoon alum. Sterilize jars and while hot pack peppers in them. Pour boiling vinegar mixture on them and seal.

We use these as hors d'oeuvres. Men, especially, are crazy about them.

Whiskey Apple Pie

Serves 6 - 8

12 oz. dried apples
1 c. bourbon
1 c. cider
1 c. brown sugar or
honey
1 t. cinnamon
1 t. ginger
1 dash nutmeg
1 9 in. uncooked pie
shell

Soak apples in bourbon and cider overnight. If apples are very dry, add more cider to barely cover and cook for 20 minutes to soften. Preheat oven to 400 degrees. Add brown sugar or honey and the spices to the apples. Place this mixture in the pie crust. Turn oven back to 350 degrees and bake 20 to 25 minutes. The pie does not need an upper crust (because of calories). It will appear flat.

Apple Pie

Serves 6

2 c. thinly sliced
apples
1 c. sugar
$\frac{1}{3}$ c. orange juice
$\frac{1}{3}$ c. mayonnaise
(melted)
1 heaping T. flour
$\frac{1}{2}$ t. nutmeg

Mix and put in a 9 inch unbaked pie shell. Bake at 400 degrees for 15 minutes, then at 250 degrees for 35 minutes.

Apple Stack Cake ——————————————— Serves 8 - 10

1 c. shortening
1 c. sugar
2 eggs
3 c. plain flour
⅓ c. cream
1 t. vanilla
½ t. salt
3 t. baking powder
Apple sauce

Mix all ingredients except apple sauce and chill. Roll out and bake in 5 layers at 350 degrees for about 15 minutes. Spread apple sauce between layers. You may use either plain apple sauce or dried apple sauce. (We prefer the dried apples.)

September was also the month when Ed picked basket after basket of ripe, sweet grapes and carried them to the cellar to make his own brand of tonic. Here are his grape wine and apple cider recipes.

Apple Cider

We picked the fine, hardly ripe winesaps to grind into cider. Ed had a beautiful cider mill and press. The pan where the juice flows was made of beautiful polished copper. The apples were carefully picked over and washed, then poured into the mill hopper and ground into a pulp, then put into the press and strained through a cloth.

Ed also made a supply of vinegar that we utilized in our pickling. He found it hard to keep sweet cider for any great length of time. He said it was just too darned good to drink. So he usually divided it into two barrels, one for hard cider and the other for vinegar.

As soon as the cider was in the barrel, a subtle change began. It began to lose its delicate flavor, some of the sugar changing to starch, and then it began to ferment, or "work." There would be a thin layer of bubbles on top. The head increased and took on a snap or zing which pleasantly tickled the tongue. After a week the alcohol content goes to 6%. If you sweeten the cider, the alcohol content goes to 11%. This is then hard cider and must be stored at 42 degrees Fahrenheit or it will soon turn to vinegar.

All the while the other barrel was placed in a room where the sun could reach it. He left this until nature took its course, and then it was ready to be spigoted out any time there was need for vinegar.

Ed's Gourmet Recipe for Blackberry Wine _____

Berries should be gathered on a fine, dry day. Wash lightly. Fermentation is started before any sugar is added, presuming any dust or impediments are left intact to aid in fermentation.

Use any amount of berries. Add enough boiling water to cover. Here you add 1 pound of sugar and ½ cup of sprite to every gallon of juice. This presumably halts all further thought of fermentation. Then the potion is bottled for future or immediate use.

Grape Wine _____

We waited until the grapes were fully ripened. Then they were at their sweetest stage. We picked them by the bushels and brought them to a place where Ed washed them, stems and all. They were packed in barrels until they fermented. This took about 72 hours. Then he racked them. This was a process of removing all stems and green grapes that accumulated at the top. You cannot strain—but after the rack was done he gave it a few hours to settle. Then he siphoned this juice into clean, sterilized 5 gallon jars. To each 5 gallons he added 2½ pounds of sugar and thoroughly dissolved it in the juice. Then he put a cork tightly in each jar. The cork had copper tubing running into a Coca-Cola bottle that had been filled ¾ full of water. This way no air or anything could touch the wine. It immediately began working. He left the wine until it quit bubbling. After it had completely quit, he siphoned the wine into bottles, which he laid on their sides; every 3 or 4 months he turned them so the wine would not die.

Norman Type Champagne (Requires no yeast) _____

Take cider that still has a very slight sparkle—about 5 or 6 days old. Rack it off through a filtering cloth, or paper, into a sterile keg that has been rinsed with scalding water. To a 10 gallon keg allow about 3 cups of the finest grain alcohol or about 2 bottles of brandy, gin or whiskey, if nothing else, and 3 pounds of sugar. Stir and let stand for 10 to 12 days with bung in loose. Now "fine" or settle the wine by the routine given below, and let settle 4 days longer—about 14 days in all. Rack carefully into champagne bottles, filtering again if at all cloudy. Cork with sound corks, and if you don't wish the risk of bombardment from inner bottle pressure, wire or tie them on tightly. Under *no* conditions use wine or other bottles. They are not made to stand high pressures. Your cellar would be filled with flying glass, for there would be an explosion. We know!

How to "Fine" or Clarify Wine _____

This recipe is dated 1736: Allow 5 egg whites and 1 tablespoon salt to each 10 gallons of wine. Beat these together into a froth; draw off 1 pint or so of wine and add to the eggs. Stir well and add this to the container of wine to be clarified. In a few days it will be "fine." From 3 to 5 days usually does the trick. The egg mixture settles out, carrying finely suspended bits of lees and sediment with it.

An Old Blackberry Wine Recipe

This recipe is over 100 years old: Gather dead-ripe berries on a dry day. Have a crock, or wood keg without head and a tap or faucet a couple of inches above bottom. Mash berries well, pour enough boiling water to cover. Let them stand with a cloth cover, for 3 to 4 days—where temperature is fairly steady and not too chilly. Pulp will rise to surface in a crust. Open tap and draw off wine in another container, and add 1 pound of sugar per gallon. Mix well in a scalded keg; let stand with bung out until it stops working. Have keg almost full. When wine stops working, drive in the bung. Rack off in 6 months and bottle, or scald keg again, return wine and let set tightly bunged for another 6 months. The latter is much better, but it is virtually impossible to have the patience to wait.

Old Dandelion Wine

2½ gals. water
6 qts. dandelion
  blooms, dry
  measure
1 T. ground ginger
3 lbs. sugar
Juice of 6 oranges
  and their grated
  peel
Juice of 6 lemons and
  their grated peel
½ cake compressed
  yeast, or 1 T.
  brewer's type
3 c. chopped raisins

Mix dandelions with water and boil for 30 minutes—timed after boiling starts. Strain, and mix with ginger, 3 pounds sugar, and grated peel of lemon and orange, then simmer another ½ hour. Pour into well-scalded stoneware crock and then add the lemon and orange juices. When lukewarm spread yeast on a piece of toast and float on top, yeasty side down, or stir in brewer's yeast. When fermentation has stopped, siphon and strain off into another well-scalded keg into which raisins have already been put. Rack off after 4 months or so, and bottle.

This recipe is dated 1677.

Spiritful Bliss

Ed assembled this concoction to serve our most prestigious guests, those whom we really wished to cater to. It is so very simple. He used:

¹/₅ gal. rye whiskey
1 jigger Jamaican rum
¹/₂ c. rock candy—
** leave in large**
** lumps**
1 doz. whole cloves
1 quartered small
** orange with peel**
** left on**
1 quartered seedless
** lemon with peel**
** left on**
Stick of cinnamon, or
** two**

Put all these ingredients in a jar and let stand for a fortnight. Strain out spices through fine cloth or filter paper. Put liquid back on fruit until needed. To serve: cut spiral orange rind and spiral lemon rind, put in whiskey glass and pour liquor over.

Grandma Tillman's Recipe for Wine _____

Work fruit (grapes or berries) down to a pulp and let stand for three days. Strain off juice (throw pulp away). To each gallon of juice add 3 pounds sugar dissolved in 1 quart water. Put crock in cool place and skim occasionally. When juice stops working and begins to taste like wine, bottle and store in a cool, dark place.

This makes a sweet wine. If you do not like it to be too sweet, use 2 pounds sugar to the quart of water and add 1 yeast cake. The quart of water and 2 pounds of sugar is for each gallon of juice. This should make your wine test from 12 to 14 percent alcohol.

Fox Grape Wine _____

Making this wine is simplicity itself. The grapes are washed and stemmed, but never crushed. Make the wine in a crock or keg. Just put 2 cups grapes in the container and cover with 1 cup sugar, then 2 more cups grapes. Cover the container but do not seal tightly, and set it in a cool, dark place. The temperature should be kept between 55 and 60 degrees. It takes about 2 months to ferment and settle out, to appear clear. At this time it should be carefully decanted into bottles and tightly capped. If you catch it at just the right time, it will still be a little sweet and have a bit of sparkle when opened.

We use grape leaves for many things. When we put our kraut to ferment in Mason jars we place a grape leaf on top. We use them for an economical main dish:

Stuffed Grape Leaves

For a stuffing put 1 cup rice in 2 cups cold water. Bring to a boil quickly, then turn to a low heat and cook until water is absorbed—about 30 minutes. Mix this partially cooked rice with ½ pound ground beef or lamb and add 1 package commercial spaghetti sauce mix. Place 1 tablespoon of the meat-rice mixture on each grape leaf and roll from the base toward the point, carefully tucking in ends. Steam the rolled grape leaves in a covered kettle for 1 hour and serve hot.

It was about this time of year that Ed and I liked to start our cheese crock. I guess there is no special way to make it; each person becomes his own master, using only his fancies and imagination.

The Cheese Crock

We start with 1 pound sharp, aged Cheddar, grated, and to it we add 1 package cream cheese and enough good olive oil to make a thick paste. Pound away at this paste in a wooden bowl until it is of spreading consistency. Add 1 teaspoon dry mustard, and a few caraway seeds, if you like caraway. Add a few jiggers of brandy or wine. We use both—this is where your talents come into play. Brandy and kirsch are a fine combination, or bourbon and port, or just Madeira. Let your imagination carry you away.

Now for the fun: When there is a piece of cheese left around, you grate it into the crock. The last drops left in wine or liquor bottles meet a similar end. Some of the old cheese should be saved to act as a "mother" when you decide to renew your crock. A variety of cheeses may be used. Roquefort is good if used sparingly. Keep the stoneware crock in the refrigerator, covered. Take out an hour before using, and serve right from the crock. Have a few hefty spreading knives. Often we brought out the Cheese Crock for our annual Christmas Party.

Edith's Dill Crock _____

Have a good supply of fresh dill on hand for this recipe. Fill a large crock (leaving room for the vegetables) with a brine made of 10 measures of water to $3/4$ measure of salt, adding, if you wish, a dollop of vinegar, but no more than $1/4$ measure for each 10 measures of water. Toss in a few cloves of garlic, but be very modest with these. Now begin packing in fresh, clean vegetables, with generous layers of dill between. Try any of the firm vegetables in your garden. Strange and marvelous things happen to green string beans if parboiled 2 to 3 minutes, just long enough to get the fuzz off, then flung into the brine-filled crock. After these have enjoyed a few days of dreamy floating in their pungent bath, add a layer of wax beans or small raw onions or baby carrots. It's fun to experiment. Raw whole pods of peas emerge sweet and crunchy. Edith uses raw cauliflower florets, cucumber chunks or little finger sized cucumbers. A handful of washed, clean grape leaves do no harm to the flavor of your dill crock. Edith also tosses in a layer of small fresh okra pods. Sometimes she tosses in a handful of cling peaches. It seems her crock has no end.

Green Tomato Catsup

This is a condiment you will not soon forget.

Slice 1 peck green tomatoes. Slice 3 large onions. Place them in layers in a crock, sprinkling salt in between, and let stand 24 hours. Drain. Put them in a kettle and add 2 cups vinegar, 3½ cups brown sugar, 1 tablespoon salt, ½ tablespoon black pepper, ½ teaspoon each of allspice, ginger, and cinnamon, and 3 tablespoons prepared mustard. Add ¾ cup pickling spices tied in a cloth bag. Boil it all for 2 hours. Strain through a sieve and bottle.

Plum and Nut Conserve

Cut 5 pounds ripe blue plums, 1 pound raisins and 1 cup walnut meats and mix with 5 pounds sugar and the juice and grated rind of 2 oranges. Let stand overnight. The next morning cook until it thickens, but don't let it become too thick. About 50 minutes of boiling usually does it. Ladle into glasses and seal with paraffin.

Brown Sugar Peaches in Port or Brandy _____

We use fresh peaches which are slightly underripe. For 6 quarts peaches make a syrup of 3 pounds brown sugar, 1 quart cider vinegar, 2 cups water, 1 sliced lemon, 3 tablespoons whole cloves, 4 sticks cinnamon and a small piece of ginger. Boil the syrup until clear and add the peaches a quart at a time, cooking until heated through or about 5 minutes after they start to boil. Pack into sterilized jars, pouring 2 ounces of good brandy or port into each quart jar. When all of the peaches are cooked, boil down the syrup slightly and pour hot over peaches and seal at once.

When these spicy peaches are served, never pour the syrup away. A good cook learns to hoard these treasures. Sometimes we use it to marinate a mushroom salad or mix with mayonnaise for a fruit salad. Or you can dribble over iced fresh fruits for desserts. It's good in a barbecue sauce.

Real Old Fashioned Brandied Cherries _____

Fill a quart jar ¾ full of well washed cherries and 1 cup sugar; then fill jar to the top with commercial brandy. Seal the jar. Set it away in a dark place and forget about it for at least 3 months. Then don't drink too much.

ED GOES HUNTING

When October came with its crisp air and frosty mornings, I saw our beautiful setter, Lady, watching Ed with impatience as he got his guns down to oil and his heavy boots to relace. She flopped on the floor and pretended to sleep, whimpering all the while as if she were dreaming of the chuck-chucking of the quail or ruffed grouse. This was her life and so was it Ed's, and I must say I enjoyed it with them. I surely relished the quail and the grouse they brought home to make delicious meals.

At first, to see the beautiful bobwhite and his mate being readied for the table took a lot of the joy out of the taste buds. The delicacy of the quail is incomparable to any other fowl. To have one killed seemed a destruction of nature's beauty. We tried to pacify our sadness by reminding ourselves of the North Carolina Wildlife Resources Commission's suggestion that quail needed to be thinned out to protect their species from overpopulation.

Our Favorite Quail

Clean and wash birds thoroughly. Cut as you do home-style chicken. We toss them in a paper bag in flour that has been salted with 2 teaspoons salt and ½ teaspoon black pepper. Fry in a black iron frying pan in ¼ cup hot Crisco. Fry at 350 degrees until brown. Then reduce heat to 200 degrees and cook slowly for about 30 minutes. Take quail out and put on paper towels to absorb shortening. Into the fat remaining in pan, stir in 4 tablespoons flour—stir until it is golden brown—then mix in milk and water to make a cream gravy. Then put quail back in and simmer 20 minutes. Be sure to have plenty of the biscuits made from the recipe below, for they melt with the gravy. Allow 1 quail per person.

Biscuits   Serves 6

2 c. flour
3 t. baking powder
1 t. salt
½ t. soda
4 T. Crisco
Buttermilk

Sift dry ingredients together. Then add Crisco and crumble with fingertips until the mixture has the consistency of meal. Using a fork, work in just enough buttermilk to make dough you can roll and cut. Bake in 400 degree oven until brown.

Stuffed Quail

Serves 8

8 cleaned quail
1½ sticks margarine
1 lb. chicken livers
2 med. onions, chopped
1 green pepper, chopped
2 cloves garlic, minced
2 c. wild rice, cooked
2 c. chicken broth
1½ c. port wine

Sew the body cavity of quail. Sauté birds in 1 stick margarine until they are browned. Place in baking dish and bake at 325 degrees for ½ hour.

Sauté livers, onions, pepper and garlic in ½ stick margarine. Do not let vegetables brown, but cook to a clear color. Add cooked rice, chicken broth and wine. Place mixture in a 3 quart baking dish. Cover and bake at 325 degrees for about 20 minutes or until liquid is absorbed. Serve quail over rice.

Variation:

For stuffing quail, break lightly toasted bread slices and mix with broken pieces of pecans, 1 stick margarine, salt and pepper to taste and a pinch of poultry seasoning. Put this stuffing in body cavity of each quail and secure with toothpick. Bake 45 minutes in a 400 degree oven.

Roast Ruffed Grouse _____ Serves 4

1 2 to 3 lb. grouse
1 bay leaf
1 clove garlic,
   crushed
Few celery leaves
1 slice lemon
4 slices bacon
Melted margarine
1 med. onion, sliced
2 4 oz. cans
   mushrooms
1 c. chicken broth

Rub grouse inside and out with salt and pepper. Place the bay leaf, garlic, celery leaves and lemon in the cavity. Tie legs together with a string. Turn wings under. Cover breast with bacon slices and a cheesecloth soaked in margarine. Place grouse breast side up in baking pan. Arrange onion slices and mushrooms, with their liquid, around grouse. Pour chicken broth over grouse. Roast in a preheated 350 degree oven for about 30 minutes per pound, or until tender. Baste frequently with liquid in pan. Remove cheesecloth and string.

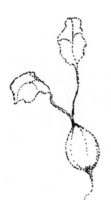

Dove Pie _____ Serves 6

This is one of the best of our game dishes. At first I resented having them killed and wasn't too fond of this pie. But it doesn't take long to realize its sweet delicacy.

6 doves, cleaned
4 c. water
1 onion, chopped
1 sm. bunch parsley, chopped
3 whole cloves
2 T. all-purpose flour
2 T. margarine
Salt and pepper
Pastry for a double crust pie

Place doves in water to cover; add onion, parsley and cloves. Cook until tender. Remove doves. Skim liquid and thicken it with a paste made of flour and margarine. Season to taste with salt and pepper. Line a baking dish with pastry and place doves in dish. Cover with the gravy. Top with pastry. Bake at 350 degrees for 1 hour.

Quail or Doves in Grape Leaves _____

Here is a really deluxe way of cooking these game birds into a gourmet dish. I rub the cleaned birds (1 per person) inside and out with a little salt and pepper. Then I fill them with a celery stuffing, then wrap each bird in 2 grape leaves and pack four of them in a glass baking dish with a tight-fitting cover. I then cream 2 sticks margarine with 1 tablespoon flour, season it with a little salt and pepper and pack around the birds. This is tightly covered and cooked about 40 minutes in a 400 degree oven.

Try this when you are giving a special dinner and watch your guests' eyes light up!

Hunting season opened October 15 for bear and wild boar hunts. Ed belonged to two large hunting clubs. Many of our clientele also belonged.

One of these clubs had thousands of acres in virgin forest leased for hunting. They went to Mt. Mitchell, where they had a small, comfortable inn at which to stay while on these trips. They almost always had good luck, plus a good time. Despite being so tired, they played poker into the wee hours of morning. They had men there who dressed their game, and then it was divided equally. The man who shot the bear got the hide to bring home to have it made into a rug or wall hanging. The hunters were always proud of the bear skin, the boar's tusks, or the deer's antlers. It gave a hunter prestige to be able to display his trophies in his game room or den.

The other club Ed went with hunted in different locations. This group enjoyed camping out. They used sleeping bags to do the little sleeping they did. The season usually opened with an all-night poker game. The dogs, on the other hand, seemed to anticipate the following day, so they curled up in a leaf bed near the campfire for the rest that they should have before tackling the snow-covered mountains.

Finally one of the other hunters would quit the game to fix breakfast so they would be ready to go just before daylight. This breakfast did not consist of the food Ed and the others had been used to at home. They had no ham, eggs, sausage and hot biscuits. Instead, they had thickly sliced rashers of salt pork, onions, cornbread they had brought with them, and delicious potato cakes John B. made.

Potato Cake Recipe à la John B. _____ Serves 6

Grate 6 large raw potatoes and stir in 3 whole eggs, 3/4 cup flour, 1/2 teaspoon salt and 2 cups milk. Fry 1/4 pound salt pork in an iron skillet until brown and drain, leaving some of the fat in the pan. Add the batter, scatter the dried salt pork over it and bake over a few coals in an iron oven; also put a few coals on top. Bake slowly until done.

Serve these big nourishing pancakes with margarine, molasses or jam. Apple sauce is a good side dish.

These pancakes were a tradition of the season, just as it was a tradition for John B. to cook the hunters' dinner at nightfall after a long day of hunting, while the men, exhausted, red-faced and rumpled, sipped highballs, yelling to John B., "For God's sake, how much longer, John B., how long?"

But roasting or stewing the grouse and rabbit and sometimes a squirrel or two was an honor John B. deserved. He knew this pot must simmer slowly. He was a large-boned, slim man, and his face took on the aspect of some woods creature as he sipped and ladled. Woodsmoke seemed to wreathe around him as he bent over the pots and oven in pious absorption, inhaling the mingled fumes of fowl, squirrel and rabbit, and butter and spices. What he at last drew forth was, surely, worth the torment of waiting. John B. was a favorite of all the hunters, not only because he was an accomplished cook but because he was an excellent hunter as well.

Here are some of Ed's and my recipes for the hunting season, along with John B's.

Venison Hash

Slice leftover venison neatly. From the odds and ends make a broth by almost covering them with water, adding a small minced onion, a dash of Kitchen Bouquet and of Worcestershire, a lump of butter, a minced clove of garlic, any leftover gravy and a squeeze of lemon juice. Simmer for about 1 hour. Drain, season and add a little currant jelly and some prepared mustard to taste. Add venison slices cut quite small and heat through only.

Ed's Game Soup   Serves 12

This is one of Ed's specialties, prepared when the men go for a weekend hunt. It is a rich, wonderful soup. After the first day's bag, he will select a pair of wild ducks, a partridge, and a medium-sized rabbit. He disjoints them and browns them in butter, along with 1 cubed lean ham, 2 chopped onions and 1 diced carrot and turnip each. A large beef soup bone with the fat all trimmed off is then added, along with seasonings and enough water to cover all. Simmer the soup several hours until the fowl or game is tender. Remove it but keep it warm. Simmer broth for another hour or so. Remove soup bone. Return the fowl and other game to pot and add a little chopped parsley and finely diced celery. Simmer until the celery is done, add some Worcestershire, 1 tablespoon tomato paste and a little sherry or Madeira and serve with a bowl of fried croutons.

Sometimes Ed used a few tablespoons wild rice. But Ed thinks a good game dinner requires more than just the bird and beast alone. Wild rice, red cabbage, ruby wine, certain tart jellies, fruits and nuts—all these are natural handmaidens.

Red Cabbage _____ Serves 6

Melt 3 tablespoons poultry fat (duck fat is ideal) or fresh bacon fat in a large kettle and in it fry 2 chopped onions for a few minutes. Add 1 head red cabbage, sliced thin, and only enough water so that it will not burn. Simmer, covered, 20 minutes; then add 2 chopped tart apples, salt, pepper, a bay leaf, 1 teaspoon caraway seed, ½ cup red wine vinegar, 3 or 4 tablespoons brown sugar to taste, and a few whole cloves. Simmer until about done, add a few tablespoons flour and boil uncovered another minute or so to reduce the liquid.

Pickled Walnuts or Butternuts _____

Shell the nuts (wild ones). Make a syrup of ½ cup white sugar, 1½ cups brown sugar, 4 cups water, 1 cup vinegar, 2 tablespoons honey, ½ teaspoon each of ginger, allspice, mustard seeds, and curry powder, and the chopped rinds of a lemon and an orange. Boil until thickened. Add 2 or 3 cups shelled nuts, simmer 5 minutes, remove from heat and add several jiggers rum. Bottle while hot.

Serve with any dark-meated fowl or game. This was always my contribution to the hunt.

Bear Roast

As soon as the roast is home and thoroughly washed, I put it in a large black iron pot and cover with the following marinade for overnight or sometimes longer: 2 cups olive oil, 3 cups wine vinegar, 4 to 5 cloves garlic (mashed), 1 tablespoon salt and 1 crushed red pepper. (This makes marinade for about an 8 to 10 pound roast.)

Take the roast out of the marinade. Brown it in 4 tablespoons margarine. Sprinkle with flour mixed with 1 teaspoon salt and 1 teaspoon black pepper. Put in a bake-and-serve bag. Preheat the oven to 500 degrees. Put the roast in for 20 minutes, then reduce heat to 300 degrees. Let the bear roast for 3 hours, or until done.

Helen's Light Corn Bread

This was the time I enjoyed making Helen A. Lewis's Light Corn Bread. For only corn bread goes with bear meat. In a large bowl mix 2 cups plain cornmeal, 1 cup plain flour, 1 teaspoon salt, 1/4 cup sugar, 1 teaspoon soda and 1 teaspoon baking powder.

Make a well in center of dry ingredients. Add 2 cups buttermilk, 1 egg and 1/2 cup shortening (do not melt shortening). Mix very quickly and put in a greased loaf pan (use the kind of pan you use for light bread). Bake at 350 degrees for 1 hour. Turn out and serve warm. Cut in slices. Any leftover bread is good fried in butter.

Two of the vegetables we think go with a bear dinner are:

Crunch Top Sweet Potatoes —————————— Serves 10

1³/₄ c. cooked mashed sweet potatoes
1 c. Cool Whip
¹/₂ c. powdered sugar
8 oz cream cheese, softened
1 t. vanilla extract
1 3 oz can coconut
¹/₄ c. chopped pecans
¹/₄ c. all purpose flour
¹/₄ c. brown sugar
2 T. margarine, melted
¹/₂ t. ground cinnamon
Dash nutmeg

Combine potatoes, Cool Whip, powdered sugar, cream cheese and vanilla in a mixing bowl. Beat with electric mixer until smooth. Place potato mixture in casserole and top with the combined remaining ingredients. Bake at 350 degrees until slightly browned.

Sautéed Fresh Turnip Greens _____ Serves 6

1 lb. fresh turnip
  greens
2 strips salt pork
1/3 c. chopped onion
1/3 c. minced green
  pepper
1 t. salt
1/4 t. black pepper
1/2 t. sugar
2 t. freshly squeezed
  lemon juice
1 hard cooked egg

Wash turnip greens thoroughly. Trim off coarse stems. Fry salt pork in heavy skillet until crispy; remove it from the drippings and set aside. Add onion and green pepper to drippings and sauté until limp. Add chopped greens to the onion and pepper. Stir to mix well. Cover tightly and cook for 10 to 15 minutes, or until tender. Add salt, black pepper, sugar and lemon juice. Toss lightly. Turn into a serving dish and crumble salt pork and hard-cooked egg on top.

To serve with the bear and sweet potatoes and greens we like this bread:

Ash Cake Bread _____

Mix 2 cups cornmeal and 1 teaspoon salt. Add enough hot water to make a stiff dough. Let stand an hour or more. With the hands, shape into cake about 1 inch thick.

Lay on hot hearthstones near the fire until the outside crusts up a little. Then cover with hot ashes and bake at least 1/2 hour or until well browned. Brush off ashes with a cloth. Split with slabs of butter and eat hot. Good!

Venison Meatballs _____ Serves 8 - 10

1 lb. ground venison
½ lb. ground pork
½ c. fine dry bread
  crumbs
1 egg, beaten
½ c. cooked mashed
  potatoes
1 t. seasoned salt
½ t. brown sugar
¼ t. black pepper
¼ t. ground allspice
¼ t. ground nutmeg
⅛ t. ground cloves
⅛ t. ground ginger
3 T. margarine

Combine all ingredients except margarine. Mix well and shape into balls about 1 inch in diameter. Melt margarine in skillet over low heat. Add meatballs and brown on all sides, shaking pan now and then. Cover tightly and cook over low heat for 15 minutes.

Okra Casserole _____ Serves 10

We always try to serve this with venison. It is nice and juicy while the venison has a tendency to be dry.

8 slices bacon
4 med. onions, sliced
2 qts. sliced okra
  (fresh or frozen)
3 green peppers,
  sliced
6 med. tomatoes,
  peeled and
  quartered
Sliced olives

Fry bacon until crisply done. Take bacon out and dry on paper towels. Then fry onion and pepper slices in drippings until limp. Alternate layers of okra and the other vegetables in a casserole. Crumble bacon and sliced olives on top. Brown lightly in oven for 30 minutes at 350 degrees.

Zeb's Venison Roast

1 venison roast
Lard
1 c. cooking oil
½ c. vinegar
2 c. red wine
1 t. salt
¼ c. chopped parsley
1 bay leaf
3 cloves garlic
1 large onion,
   chopped coarsely
1 T. black pepper

Trim all fat from venison and then lard the venison. Mix remaining ingredients for a marinade. Marinate roast in a bake-and-serve bag 2 or 3 days. Punch holes in top of bag; do not allow marinade to drain out. Start roast in a 500 degree oven (preheated). Turn the oven down to 350 degrees and bake for 45 minutes per pound.

Hunting was almost Ed's way of life. It seemed to make no difference to him which game he hunted, just so the game was wild. The raccoon was almost extinct in western North Carolina. Ed helped to form a "Coon Club." They got permission to transfer the coon from eastern North Carolina to the mountains. They went to the Dismal Swamp and made arrangements with men there to trap them, and they hauled them by the truckload to our mountains. In a year or so we began to have plenty of coon for the men to hunt. After Ed had hunted several nights—all night—he had three large fat coons for Charlotte to cook for our fall guests who had come to see our beautiful array of colored leaves. They raved over this recipe:

Charlotte's Sweet Potatoes with Coon _____

Dress coon and soak for one hour in vinegar solution (mild). Drain. Cut coon into serving pieces. Salt and pepper coon and cover with water. Add a dash of cayenne pepper, some chopped garlic, celery, onions and green pepper, and boil until partially tender. Remove from heat and drain. Brown the coon in a small amount of shortening, then place in a roasting pan. Make a thin gravy with flour and drippings; pour over coon in roasting pan. Place peeled sweet potatoes around coon and bake at 350 degrees until potatoes are done.

Occasionally, by sheer luck, Ed saw a wild turkey. They are few and far between. One day he and some guests were in the wild woods. One of the men saw and followed a turkey gobbler for miles. Finally he had a chance to shoot him. They came home carrying the gobbler on their backs as if it weighed a ton. It was an 18 pound gobbler.

Most of the wild turkeys I recall having, my Uncle Zeb brought from Whiteside Cove by horseback. It was always a joyful scene to see him come riding up the lane with a huge 25 pound wild gobbler hanging on one side of his horse. It almost seemed to weigh the horse down. He always arranged to arrive in time for my mother to prepare and cook the turkey for our Thanksgiving dinner. Uncle Zeb always spent two nights. He and my father charmed my brothers, sisters and me, spinning hunting tales and tales of hardship as we sat with wide-open eyes and ears to miss not a single word.

To prepare and cook a wild turkey, we used the following recipe:

Wild Turkey

Dry pick and singe wild turkey. Wash in warm water to cover that has 4 teaspoons soda added to it. Remove tendons. Soak the turkey in salt water (4 tablespoons salt to a gallon of water) for 3 to 3½ hours. Pour off salt water, wash turkey, and rub well with lemon juice. Make a paste of butter and flour—8 to 10 tablespoons butter to 1 cup flour. Spread paste over turkey. Place bird in a 475 to 500 degree oven and brown quickly to set the paste. Stuff bird with Wild Turkey Stuffing (see below). Place in a roaster with 1 cup hot water. Cover and bake at 325 degrees for 30 minutes to the pound. When turkey is tender, remove cover and brown. Make gravy from drippings when bird is done.

Wild Turkey Stuffing

4 c. bread crumbs
  (half corn bread
  and half biscuits
  and light bread)
4 c. diced celery
1 c. chopped onion
2 T. freshly squeezed
  lemon juice
1 t. salt
1/4 t. red pepper
  (crushed)
1/2 t. Worcestershire
  sauce
1/2 t. steak sauce
1 1/2 c. butter

Combine bread crumbs, celery, onion, lemon juice, salt and red pepper. Blend Worcestershire sauce and steak sauce with butter and add to mixture.

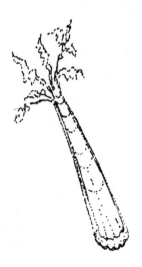

Here is a recipe for leftover turkey—if you have any.

Turkey Intrigue _____

1½ lbs. boiled turkey
  or chicken, diced
3 qts. white sauce
½ c. cooking sherry
3 pimientos
1 lb. mushroom
  pieces (canned)
1 onion, finely
  chopped or grated
2 T. salt
1 t. celery salt
2 qts. hot, cooked
  rice
1½ lbs. American
  cheese, grated

To the white sauce add sherry, chopped pimientos, sautéed chopped mushrooms, onion and seasonings. Place diced turkey in a casserole. Pour white sauce over turkey. Sprinkle rice on top and grated cheese over rice. Bake in a very slow oven (250 degrees) for 20 minutes. Serve hot.

BUTCHERING TIME

It was November. All the water pipes were made secure for the heavy freezes we anticipated. Every crack was filled to keep out the north wind.

It was at this time that Ed watched the sky and carried his butchering tools out of the smokehouse. Then he turned to me and said, "After this blow it will turn crisp and cold and our meat will keep." This meant he was thinking of the butchering, which was one of our greatest chores of the year.

Long before daybreak the next morning, the fire was crackling under the large steel barrels of water. When the water came to a boil, each fat hog was shot and bled. One by one they were brought in and plunged into the barrel of boiling water, then put on boards that Ed had placed on a platform for the scraping of the hogs. Then each hog was hung and cut down the middle so that the entrails fell into large wash pots. He had women there to clean the casings for sausage and chitterlings. The hams and bacon were put in the smokehouse to drain overnight; then came the curing process. Here is my father's recipe for curing ham:

Curing Ham

Kill hog and let stand or hang overnight. Cut up. Mix well 2 cups salt, 1 cup brown sugar, 2 tablespoons black pepper and 1 tablespoon cayenne pepper. With your hands, rub this mixture well into the ham, as much as it will possibly take, especially around the joints. Wrap securely with brown paper; tie; wrap again with brown paper. Hang up in a white meal sack in a good place to drip and also to have plenty of air. Be sure to hang the ham as the hog stands.

We used this same recipe for curing bacon, side meat, and sometimes a shoulder. However, we saved a lot of the shoulder meat for the sausage, along with any scraps of lean meat.

No other ham ever cured is as good as one cured by this method.

Leaf Lard

The choicest lard was made from the thick sheaf of fat that encases the hog's entrails. The lard was rendered and pressed dry so the fat came out. We often used our grape press to do this. Then these bits of small pieces were removed, and these were what we used to make the best bread ever put on a table.

Pork Sausage

We usually ground the meat from 4 or 5 shoulders and all excess lean meat. Then we seasoned it with salt, black pepper, crushed red peppers and sage to taste. The women worked this all up by hand. After testing to see if they had the required seasonings, they made the mixture into balls, fried them in a black iron fry pan, and canned them in hot sterilized jars, pouring the excess fat over them and sealing tightly. We served this to our summer boarders.

Not half our work was finished with the hog killing. We made the following recipes:

Scrapple
Serves 8

1 lb. pork
   (inexpensive bone
   cut)
2 pig feet
1 qt. boiling salted
   water
²/₃ c. cornmeal
1 c. cold water
Salt and pepper to
   taste
Crushed red pepper

Wash pork and pig feet well until they are thoroughly cleaned, then place in boiling salted water. Cover and simmer until meat can be easily removed from the bones. Remove meat from broth; shred, grind or cut in tiny pieces. Bring broth to boil again. Mix together cornmeal and cold water. Stir into boiling broth. Then cook and stir until thick. Season to taste with salt and pepper and a small amount of crushed red pepper. Add meat and cook for about 5 minutes. Turn into a greased loaf pan. Chill. Then cut into slices and fry until crisp and brown. Serve hot.

Souse Meat

Place a thoroughly cleaned hog's head with 4 cleaned hog's feet in a kettle of boiling water. Cook until the meat drops from the bones. Mince meat finely and place in mixing bowl. Add ¼ teaspoon black pepper, ¼ t. cayenne, ½ teaspoon crushed sage, ½ cup vinegar and 2 cups broth from which the fat has been skimmed. Mix well. Put in a loaf pan and refrigerate until firm. This slices nicely. Serve cold.

Liver Mush

Liver mush is similar to liver pudding. You cook the liver and the head separately in salted water until tender. Grind them together. In the meantime, cook some cornmeal in the broth used to cook the liver. Then mix the meats and cooked cornmeal together. Pour into pans and allow to gel or become firm.

Country Ham—Baked

Soak a 10 to 12 pound country ham in cold water to cover overnight. Preheat the oven to 500 degrees.

Scrub the ham to remove pepper coating and any mold. Place the ham in a covered roaster with 6 cups cold water. Close all vents. Bake ham 20 minutes. Turn oven off. Allow ham to remain in oven without opening door for 3 hours. Turn oven heat to 500 degrees and leave 15 minutes. Turn off heat and allow ham to remain in oven for at least 3 hours or more, or ham can be left overnight.

Remove ham from roaster and cut off rind. Ham is ready to eat. Slice thinly.

This recipe is so good with the ham:

Baked Squash _____ Serves 8

12 sm. yellow squash
1 sm. diced onion
Butter for sauté
$\frac{1}{2}$ c. cream
$\frac{1}{4}$ c. saltine crackers,
    crushed
2 T. butter

Slice squash, boil in salted water until done. Drain and mash. Sauté onions in butter. Mix squash, onion and cream together. Pour into greased casserole and top with cracker crumbs and dots of butter. Bake at 400 degrees for about $\frac{1}{2}$ hour, or until firm.

We always were happy when all the work of butchering was behind us. We knew we had plenty of pork products to do us. Then we began buying fresh hams from neighbors to cure for our summer boarders. We always froze a small amount of the pork loins, sausage, etc. We never liked to leave pork in the freezer longer than three months.

Barbecued Pork Chops _____ Serves 8

**8 loin or shoulder
pork chops 1 in.
thick**

**1 8 oz. can tomato
sauce**

½ c. catsup

½ c. water

¼ c. vinegar

1 t. salt

1 t. celery seed

⅛ t. ground cloves

½ t. Tabasco sauce

**1 T. prepared
mustard**

1 med. onion, sliced

**1 clove garlic,
crushed**

Cut a little fat from pork chops, heat in skillet, then brown meat in it (about 10 minutes). Place chops in shallow baking dish (13 x 9 x 2) one layer deep.

Pour off fat from skillet. Combine remaining ingredients; mix with browned particles in skillet. Pour over chops.

Bake uncovered in moderate oven (350 degrees) for 1 hour and 15 minutes. Turn once during baking. Adjust time for thicker or thinner chops. If you like a little "bite" in sauce, sprinkle in a little red pepper.

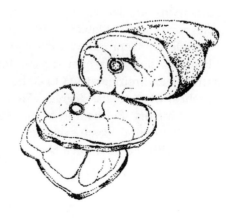

Pork Sausage with Fried Apples _____ Serves 6

2 lbs. pork sausage
3 c. sliced, unpeeled red apples
1/2 c. brown sugar
1/4 t. cinnamon
Dash ground cloves

Shape sausage into 18 balls or patties. Pan fry over low heat until no trace of pink shows. Drain once during cooking, reserving drippings. Keep hot.

Place 1/2 cup sausage drippings in skillet with tight-fitting lid. Add apples; sprinkle with brown sugar. Cover and cook slowly until apples are almost tender—15 to 20 minutes. Remove cover. Cook until apples are glazed. Sprinkle with cinnamon and cloves. Serve sausage and apples on a large platter.

Roast Fresh Pork Ham _____

To make a marinade, combine 1 1/2 cups beer, 1/2 teaspoon salt, 1 tablespoon mustard, 1 teaspoon ground ginger, 3 tablespoons soy sauce, 1/8 teaspoon hot pepper sauce, 2 tablespoons sugar, 4 tablespoons your favorite marmalade (we prefer apple or plum), 2 cloves minced garlic.

Have a whole pork ham at room temperature. Place in marinade and refrigerate 24 to 48 hours.

Preheat oven to 450 degrees. Remove ham from marinade. Wipe dry. Put ham in oven, allowing 30 to 45 minutes to the pound. Baste every 1/2 hour with part of marinade or with the traditional beer.

Serve with any of the following accompaniments.

Pan Gravy _____

Remove meat from pan (keep meat hot). Pour off all but 2 tablespoons drippings. Blend in 2 tablespoons flour. Stir well until flour is thickened and slightly browned. Add the degreased pan juices and enough milk combined with beer to make a smooth gravy. Add salt, pepper, dried herbs and grated lemon rind. Serve with fresh pork ham.

Tommye's Rhubarb Crunch _____ Serves 10

4 c. sliced rhubarb
1½ c. sugar
4 T. flour
½ c. brown sugar
½ c. flour
½ c. rolled oats
½ c. margarine

Place rhubarb in baking dish. Combine sugar and 4 tablespoons flour; sprinkle over rhubarb. Blend remaining ingredients. Sprinkle over rhubarb. Bake at 300 degrees for 1 hour.

Lima-Mushroom Supreme _____ Serves 10

8 T. butter
6 T. flour
4 c. milk
¼ c. Durkees Sauce
Worcestershire to
taste
1 c. grated cheese
24 oz. canned
mushrooms
1½ lb. pkg. limas
3 hard boiled eggs,
chopped in hunks
Salt, pepper and
tabasco to taste
Bread crumbs

Make a cream sauce with butter, flour and milk. Add Durkees Sauce. Season generously with Worcestershire. Mix next 5 ingredients in a casserole or baking dish. Add cream sauce and cover with bread crumbs. Cook in moderate oven (350 degrees) until crumbs are brown (about 30 minutes).

Chitterlings

Chitterlings are the intestines of the hog. It is important to remove all excess fat and clean them thoroughly. After boiling until tender, the chitterlings may be drained, dipped in cornmeal and fried, or dipped in a batter made of 2 cups flour, 2 eggs and 1½ cups milk, and deep fried.

This is a chitterlings recipe given to me by a Mississippi man who relished them:

10 lbs. chitterlings
Lemon juice
Salt to taste
1 T. cider vinegar
Seasoning salt to taste
1 onion, finely chopped
1 clove garlic, minced
3 bay leaves
Vinegar
Hot sauce

Place chitterlings in a basin and add cold water, a little lemon juice, and salt. Clean chitterlings thoroughly, removing as much fat as possible.

Add cold water to cover, the juice of 1 lemon, the 1 tablespoon vinegar, seasoning salt, onion, garlic and bay leaves. Bring to a boil. Cover and simmer until chitterlings are thoroughly tender. It takes about 4 hours. Serve hot with vinegar and hot sauce on the side.

Along with our innkeeping, we began to spread out. Ed loved cattle and liked growing food for them. He became so intensely interested he began to build a herd of dairy cows along with the cattle he grew for beef for our summer boarders. We bought several hundred acres for pasture land to grow the beef cattle. Also, he built a very modern, sanitary milking barn. We sold our milk to Biltmore Dairy Farms. They came to pick the milk up each day. Everything went smoothly for about four years. Then a snow storm came suddenly, cutting off our electricity. It is an ordeal to milk 30 cows by hand—we had always used electric milkers. On this cold, snowy day, Ed, our farm worker, and I finished milking at one o'clock in the afternoon. Our arms were swollen. It was a task we never imagined we could finish. After contacting our electric company we learned all the county, even the hospital, was without electricity. It was then Ed decided we were going out of the dairy business. We sold cows for as little as $82 each. They had cost us $400 each. This was a great loss we had never anticipated and one that was hard to recover from.

Besides enjoying the wonderful whole milk and whipped cream, we used to make the most delicious products from ice creams to cottage cheese. I'd like to give my cottage cheese recipe.

_____

Cottage Cheese

Take a crockful of clabbered milk. Set it on the stove to heat a little. When the whey and clabber separate, pour the curds in a jelly bag and hang it up where it will drain till dry. Season with salt, a piece of butter or rich cream. Use some pepper if desired. Mix with your hands. Serve in small balls as a salad or, if you have quite an amount, serve in a dish. Or use in the following recipe:

Scrambled Eggs (for 2)

2 T. butter
4 eggs
¾ c. cottage cheese (dry)
½ t. salt
Fresh ground or cracked pepper

Melt the butter in a skillet and remove from fire. Break the eggs into the skillet and beat with a fork. Add cottage cheese and salt. Return to the heat and cook over low heat, stirring constantly. Sprinkle with fresh ground or cracked pepper and serve.

Ed took our cattle early in the spring to the pasture range. He also had to take loads of hay for them. It was a rewarding experience to watch them grow. Always he grain-fed the young beef he expected to butcher. Here are some of the recipes we used for our beef:

Pot Roast ————————————————— Serves 10

3 T. flour
2 t. salt
¼ t. freshly ground
   black pepper
1 4 lb. bottom round
   roast of beef
3 T. bacon drippings
   or oil
½ c. freshly grated
   horseradish or
   prepared drained
   horseradish (4 oz.
   jar)
1 c. whole cranberry
   sauce
1 stick cinnamon
4 whole cloves
1 c. beef broth
16 sm. onions or
   shallots
1 bunch carrots, cut
   in 3 in. lengths

Mix flour with salt and pepper and dredge the meat in the mixture. Rub the mixture into all surfaces.

Heat bacon drippings or oil in a heavy Dutch oven or casserole and brown the meat on all sides very well over high heat. Pour off drippings into a skillet and reserve.

Mix together the horseradish, cranberry sauce, cinnamon, cloves and broth and add to meat.

Bring mixture to boil, cover tightly and simmer gently about 2 hours, or until the meat is barely tender.

Meanwhile, brown the onions in the reserved drippings in the skillet. Add carrots and cook 2 minutes longer. Drain from the fat and add to the meat broth. Cover and cook about 25 minutes longer, or until vegetables and meat are tender. The gravy is delicious over noodles.

Famous Italian Spaghetti Sauce _____ Serves 8

2 garlic cloves,
  minced
½ c. onion, chopped
3 T. olive oil
1½ lb. ground beef
1 6 oz. can tomato
  paste
1 8 oz. can tomato
  sauce
1 1 lb. can tomato
  purée
2 t. sugar
1 c. water
¼ c. parsley,
  chopped
1 sm. bay leaf
¼ t. rosemary
¼ t. basil
¼ t. thyme
¼ t. allspice
¼ t. oregano
¼ t. pepper
1 t. salt
1 4 oz. can undrained
  mushrooms

In a large saucepan cook ground beef with garlic and onion in olive oil until onions are golden brown. Add remaining ingredients, cover, and simmer gently for 2 hours or longer. Serve over spaghetti, topped with Meatballs (below).

Meatballs ————————————————— Serves 8

1 lb. ground beef
½ lb. bulk pork
  sausage
2 T. onion, chopped
2 T. celery leaves,
  chopped
½ c. dry bread
  crumbs
¼ c. milk
1 egg
½ t. salt
½ t. pepper
1 clove garlic, minced
¼ c. Parmesan cheese

Combine ingredients; shape into 1 inch balls. Brown; drain fat. Add to sauce and simmer 30 minutes. Serve over spaghetti.

Chateaubriand ————————————————— Serves 8

3 lb. sirloin, cut 3 in.
  thick
Meat tenderizer
½ c. beef broth
1 c. dry wine
4 oz. butter
3 t. lemon juice
½ t. freshly ground
  pepper
¼ c. chives, minced
¼ c. parsley, minced
1 4 oz. can sliced
  mushrooms

Sprinkle meat with tenderizer. Pierce all surfaces at 1 inch intervals with fork. Cover and refrigerate overnight. Cook over charcoal grill six inches from coals, allowing 20 minutes for each side. Meanwhile, combine other ingredients except chives, parsley and mushrooms. Bring to boil; reduce heat and simmer until butter melts. Add herbs and mushrooms. Some of this sauce may be used to baste meat while cooking. Carve meat across grain in thin slices (diagonal). Serve with sauce.

Beef Stroganoff _____ Serves 8

1½ lbs. round,
   sirloin or chuck
   steak, cut in ¾ in.
   squares
Flour
2 T. shortening
½ onion, chopped
1 clove garlic, minced
1 c. mushrooms,
   sliced
½ to 1 can condensed
   tomato soup or
   bouillon
1 c. sour cream
⅓ t. Worcestershire
   sauce
½ t. salt
⅛ t. pepper, freshly
   ground
6 - 8 drops Tabasco or
   1½ t. prepared
   mustard
Parsley, chives or
   dill, chopped, for
   garnish

Dip meat in flour. (Flour may be seasoned if desired.) Brown in shortening and add onion, garlic and mushrooms. Cook slowly for a few minutes. Combine remaining ingredients; pour over meat. Cover and simmer 1 hour or until tender. Serve over cooked rice. Garnish with herbs as desired.

When we'd butcher a beef we tried using every part of it on our tables, learning to turn the less expensive cuts into desirable dishes. Thus we came up with:

Stuffed Flank Burgundy

Serves 4

1½ - 2 lb. flank steak
Flour
Salt and pepper to
  taste
2 c. prepared stuffing
½ c. celery, finely
  chopped
½ c. sweet pickle
  relish
¼ c. oil or melted
  margarine
1 can condensed
  onion soup
½ c. Burgundy,
  bouillon or other
  wine

Score steak on both sides. Dredge meat in flour, salt and pepper. Combine stuffing, celery and relish; spread on steak. Roll up like a jelly roll; fasten with toothpicks or sew with dental floss. Brown well in oil or margarine. Add soup and wine; simmer covered 2 hours.

Braised Beef _____ Serves 4 - 5

⅓ c. flour
Salt and pepper
2 lbs. lean round
   steak 1 in. thick
3 T. bacon fat
1 can condensed
   tomato soup
½ c. sherry
1 sm. onion, minced
½ c. sour cream
2 T. parsley, chopped
1 sm. can mushrooms

Mix flour, salt and pepper; rub into the meat. Pound in flour with mallet or edge of heavy plate. Cut meat into thin strips 2 inches long. Brown meat in fat; add soup, sherry and onion. Simmer covered for 1 hour and 15 minutes or until meat is tender. Add remaining ingredients. Heat thoroughly.

American Beef and Peppers _____ Serves 6

1 lb. round steak, cut
   in thin strips
3 T. oil
1 can mushroom
   soup
1 can water
Accent to taste
Salt and pepper to
   taste
1 large green pepper,
   sliced in rings
1 large onion, sliced
4 c. steamed rice

Brown meat in oil in heavy skillet; add soup, water and seasonings. Simmer covered over low heat about 20 minutes. Additional water may be added if needed to keep the liquid the consistency of rich gravy. Add pepper rings and onion slices to meat and continue cooking until tender. Serve over rice.

Sirloin Tips ———————————————— Serves 8

3 lbs. sirloin tips, cut in 1 in. cubes
3 T. butter
1 3 oz. can tomato paste
2 T. wine vinegar
1 c. Burgundy
½ stick cinnamon
2 bay leaves
1 lb. tiny whole onions, peeled
1 t. salt
½ t. pepper
1 t. cornstarch
¼ c. water

Place meat in deep saucepan with butter. Simmer over medium heat, stirring constantly, until meat is tender; mix in tomato paste, vinegar and wine. Add remaining ingredients except cornstarch and water; simmer covered for 1 hour. Mix cornstarch and water, blend into sauce.

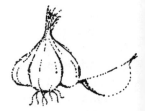

My Favorite Stew _____ Serves 10

1½ lb. chuck, cubed
4 T. flour
2 T. fat
3 T. onion, chopped
1 clove garlic
¼ c. water
1½ c. canned
   tomatoes
1½ t. Accent
1 bay leaf
4 t. salt
⅛ t. pepper
6 carrots
4 potatoes, quartered
1½ c. green beans,
   cut in 1 in. lengths
6 sm. white onions

Roll meat in flour; brown in fat in a large pot. Add chopped onion, garlic, water, tomatoes and seasonings; cover. Simmer over low heat for 1 hour and 30 minutes; add vegetables. Cook 30 minutes longer or until vegetables and meat are tender.

Short Ribs of Beef Dinner _____ Serves 10

**5 lbs. short ribs, cut
   in 2 in. pieces**
4 T. flour
1 t. salt
½ t. pepper
3 T. bacon drippings
¾ c. onion, chopped
1 c. Burgundy wine
1 c. beef bouillon
½ t. thyme
**1 t. Worcestershire
   sauce**
12-16 sm. potatoes
**12-16 sm. carrots,
   cleaned**
1 sm. can mushrooms
Parsley for garnish

Dredge meat in flour, salt and pepper. Brown in bacon drippings. Add onion; sauté 5 minutes. Add wine, bouillon and thyme. Cover; simmer 2 to 2½ hours. Add remaining ingredients and some water if necessary. Cook covered for 45 minutes or until tender. Note: Vegetables may also be boiled in separate pan and seasoned with butter and salt.

To serve, arrange vegetables around ribs; sprinkle with parsley.

Broiled Filet Mignon _____ Serves 2

2³/₄ lbs. beef filets
2 bananas, halved
   lengthwise
¹/₂ c. plus 2 T. butter
1 T. flour
1 c. milk
1¹/₂ t. salt
Pepper
¹/₂ c. prepared
   mustard
¹/₂ c. prepared
   horseradish
2 drops
   Worcestershire
   sauce

Broil filets briefly on each side. Sauté bananas on both sides in 2 tablespoons butter; set aside. Stir in remaining butter, flour and milk; bring to a boil. Reduce heat; add remaining ingredients. Cook a moment longer. Arrange filets on a platter; surround with bananas and cover with the sauce.

Savory Roast Beef _____ Serves 8 - 10

4 lbs. boneless rump
   or round roast,
   sliced
Salt and pepper
1¹/₂ sticks of
   margarine
6 - 8 large onions,
   sliced
Mushrooms, halved
1 t. Worcestershire
¹/₄ c. water

Season roast with salt and pepper; brown each slice in margarine. Sauté onions in meat drippings. In a Dutch oven alternate layers of meat, onions and mushrooms. Add Worcestershire sauce and water. Cover and bake at 350 degrees for 2 hours or until tender.

Burgundy Beef Brisket _____ Serves 10

3 - 4 lbs. brisket of
  beef
3 T. bacon fat
2 med. onions, sliced
1 beef bouillon cube
  dissolved in 1 c.
  boiling water
3 T. flour
1/2 c. catsup
1 T. Kitchen Bouquet
2 t. salt
1/2 t. thyme
1/4 t. garlic
1 c. Burgundy
2 T. sherry

Brown beef in bacon fat in large kettle. Remove beef; sauté onions in drippings until transparent. Return meat to kettle. Mix bouillon, flour, catsup and Kitchen Bouquet; pour over meat. Add seasonings, garlic and wines; simmer for 3 hours or until very tender. Small potatoes and carrots may be added the last 30 minutes of cooking.

Stuffing Meat Loaf _____ Serves 12

1 sm. can tomato
  juice
1 egg
1 t. salt
2 lbs. ground chuck
1 8 oz. pkg. dried
  stuffing mix
1/4 lb. margarine
8 large mushroom
  slices
Butter

Combine tomato juice, egg, salt, meat and 1 cup stuffing mix. Prepare remaining stuffing mix according to package directions. Place meat mixture in 9 x 9 pan; top with stuffing. Bake at 375 degrees for 45 minutes. Top with mushrooms sautéed in butter.

Beef Potato House Pie _____ Serves 6

2 lbs. ground beef
Salt and pepper to
   taste (for meat)
1 large green pepper,
   chopped
1 large onion,
   chopped
6 large potatoes,
   peeled
Salt and pepper to
   taste (for potatoes)
Butter
Milk
American cheese,
   grated

Brown the meat with seasonings, green pepper and onion. Skim off excess grease. Boil the potatoes; drain. Whip to a smooth consistency, adding salt, pepper, butter and milk. Make alternating layers of beef mixture and potatoes in a casserole. Top with grated cheese. Heat in a 375 degree oven for 20 to 30 minutes.

Yum–Yum _____

Amounts can be adjusted; a pound of ground beef will serve 4 persons. For each pound of ground beef, plan to use 1 cup coarsely chopped onion, 1 cup chopped celery, $1/2$ chopped green pepper, 1 can mushroom soup diluted with $1/2$ can water, and a 3 ounce can chow mein noodles. Brown meat to a crisp brown in some margarine while onions, celery and pepper are browning in some oil to pale gold. Season meat lightly with salt and pepper and combine with vegetables in a casserole. Rinse out both pans with a little water to get all juices; pour over casserole and add diluted soup. Cover and bake in a 350 degree oven for 45 minutes. Remove cover, spread chow mein noodles on top and allow to heat through.

PICNICS AND PARTIES

In the innkeeping business you had to allow for many things you didn't anticipate. Some days the cook did not appear, waitresses decided it was time for a day on the town, or some very important person among the personnel was sick. It was times like this that Ed was always willing to promote an outdoor adventure. It might have been a trip to Whiteside Mountain, a visit to the Blue Ridge Parkway, a trip to Cherokee or the Smokies, or a journey to numerous other places. He could nearly always persuade the guests to take a trip for a picnic they would not soon forget. They were always ready for a repeat.

While Ed talked to the guests, Maggie Belle (one cook) and I were preparing the things he must take. They took blankets or plastic sit-upons, two card tables for serving, one large barbecue grill, charcoal, lighter fluid, heavy plastic plates, a roll of paper towels, a large plastic bag for trash and plastic knives and forks. The things he served were finger foods or "do it yourself" types.

One of Ed's Menus was:

*Tender ears of corn in the husks
(always allow 2 for each person)
Large shrimp (unpeeled)—1 pound per person
Hot Dogs and Buns
Vegetable Salad
Iced Canned Beverages*

Grilled Corn

Soak unhusked corn on cob in a large container of water for as long as possible. Grill in husks over charcoal, turning frequently. When outside is dry, even lightly scorched, it is done. Melt stick of butter in pie pan on grill. Each person peels his own corn, rolls in butter, salts—it's delicious. Ed says it was always the hit of the picnic!

Shrimp

Plan 1 pound per person. Use the large size because they are more easily peeled and eaten under casual circumstances. As soon as charcoal is burning well, place a large container of water on to boil. When boiling well, add a couple cans of beer, then add shrimp. Cook 3 minutes. Serve with melted butter sprinkled with garlic salt or bring along your favorite seafood sauce. The shrimp are great right out of the pot and each person peels his own.

Hot Dogs and Buns ————————————————

Whoever heard of a picnic without them? Simply let each person broil his own over the dying coals as he is ready to eat them. These should be served after the corn and shrimp are done. Ed takes several long handled barbecue forks, catsup, mustard relish and cut-up sweet onions.

Vegetable Salad ————————————————

Ahead of time, wash vegetables and cut up and store in sandwich bags with ice to maintain crispness. Peel and cut carrot sticks; cut celery in 4 inch sticks; slice cucumbers (do not peel); section cauliflower into bite-sized pieces; and slice zucchini and yellow squash in ¼ inch slices.

Serve chilled and mixed on paper platters with bottled Catalina French Dressing.

Sometimes we had a large picnic on the lawn. These, too, went over big.

Menu for Lawn Picnic

Pickled Mushrooms   Sardine Dip
Sliced Cold Ham and Turkey
Potato Salad   Marinated 3 Bean Salad
Deviled Eggs   Baked Eggplant
Blender Orange and Cranberry Mold
Assorted Breads   Orange Cup Cakes
Coffee   Iced Tea   Milk

Here is one recipe for bread we used:

Louise's Yum Yum Corn Bread _____ Serves 6

**1 c. self-rising
   cornmeal**
⅓ c. Mazola corn oil
2 eggs
1 c. sour cream
**1 sm. can creamed
   style corn**
1 t. sugar

Bake in preheated 400 degree oven in a well greased pan.

For years we saved the gleanings of Ed's expensive but delightful hunts for a special dinner and to these we invited our special guests, our dearest friends. We brought out our special Rum Pot that had been working for about 7½ months. We also added a new dish each year or so. Usually it was at Christmas.

Menu

Rum Pot
Bolo Crabmeat   Chutney Dip
Chicken Wings with Zippy Dip
Boiled Slaw
Doves   Quail   Wild Turkey   Wild Boar
Zeb's Venison Roast   Bear Roast
Turnip, Mustard and Poke Greens, Mixed
Pea Pods with Shallots   Corn Pone
Biscuits   Wine
Fruits   Southern Pecan Pie   Cake

Here are some of the recipes; the others will be found elsewhere in this book.

Bolo Crabmeat _____ Serves 4

1 lb. crabmeat
1 shredded cucumber
¼ c. chopped parsley
¼ c. chopped green onion
½ c. mayonnaise
½ c. grapefruit juice
Juice of 1 lemon
Chopped parsley for garnish

Combine all ingredients except parsley for garnish. Let stand in refrigerator 2 hours; drain. Arrange in bowl; garnish with chopped parsley. Surround with crackers or melba toast rounds.

Chutney Dip

4 eggs, hard boiled
1 3 oz. pkg. cream
  cheese
1 T. Worcestershire
1 T. curry powder
Dash cayenne
2 - 3 dashes Tabasco
¼ t. celery seeds
2 T. mayonnaise
Salt and pepper to
  taste
3 - 4 T. bottled
  chutney

Mash eggs with cream cheese. Add other ingredients, blending well, adding chutney last. Chill.

Wild Boar

Cut meat in small thin chunks (3 inch long). Season well with cracked pepper. Dip chunks in Sweet Sour Sauce (below) and barbecue over hot coals, basting frequently. Cook 2 - 3 hours. The meat will be tender and sweet.

Sweet Sour Sauce

1 T. dry mustard
3 T. garlic-flavored
   red wine vinegar
$^1/_2$ c. catsup
1 t. horseradish
1 T. cornstarch
2 - 3 T. brown sugar
$^1/_4$ t. curry powder
$^3/_4$ c. pineapple juice
Salt and pepper to
   taste
2 T. soy sauce

Mix all ingredients together thoroughly. Cook until slightly thickened and clear. If too thick, add more pineapple juice. Serve hot or chilled.

Turnip, Mustard and Poke Greens, Mixed

We froze these greens separately. When we had large dinners we combined them and added them to a kettle that was already filled half full of generous rashers of salt pork already boiling. We salted to taste and cooked until tender.

Pea Pods with Shallots

We used our home-grown sugar peas with the edible pods. We started them to cook in a little water. We added sautéed tiny white shallots and a few sliced pimientos for color. Then we stirred in a small can of sliced water chestnuts, butter and salt and pepper to taste, and served them hot.

Chicken Wings with Zippy Dip

Have your butcher unjoin wings. Wash the cut-off tips of wings and pat dry with paper towels. Sprinkle with garlic salt. Dip wing tips in an egg batter. In a bag, mix flour, corn flakes, bread crumbs, nutmeg and red pepper. Shake batter-coated wing tips in this bag until well coated. Fry in deep fryer. Serve with Zippy Dip (below).

Zippy Dip

1 pt. sour cream
⅓ c. pickle relish
1 3 oz. pkg.
** Roquefort cheese**
2 t. mustard
Dash Tabasco sauce
Dash Worcestershire
Dash curry powder

Blend all ingredients together. Serve in a bowl. Dip fried golden brown chicken wing tip into dip.

Party Pick-Ups

Cheese Fondue _____ Serves 6

**6 slices of bread cut
in squares**
**¹/₂ lb. sharp cheddar
cheese (grated)**
6 eggs, beaten
2 c. milk
**1 stick margarine
(melted)**
Salt

Put alternate layers of bread and cheese—beginning with a layer of bread—on bottom of baking pan. Pour eggs and milk that have been mixed together over pan, then add melted margarine and a pinch of salt. Let stand in refrigerator for at least 4 hours. Bake at 400 degrees for 40 minutes. You may double or triple this recipe. It's good to make early in the morning and take out of the refrigerator just in time for the meal. It is a tried and true luncheon dish, as good as any cheese soufflé.

Stuffed Mushrooms _____ Serves 8 - 10

½ c. white bread
  crumbs
12 large mushrooms
2 cloves garlic, finely
  minced
2 T. chopped parsley
Salt and freshly
  ground black
  pepper to taste
2 eggs
½ c. ricotta cheese
¼ c. olive oil
¼ c. freshly grated
  Parmesan cheese

Preheat oven to 400 degrees.

Soak bread crumbs in a little water. Then squeeze dry and place in mixing bowl.

Chop the mushroom stems and add to bread crumbs along with garlic, parsley, salt, pepper, eggs and ricotta cheese. Blend well. Stuff mushroom caps with filling and arrange them cap side down, on a dish rubbed lightly with a little olive oil. Combine remaining oil and Parmesan and sprinkle over mushrooms. Bake 20 minutes.

Toasted Pumpkin Seed _____

When you have cut a pumpkin, remove seeds and wash thoroughly, then put them in the sun to dry. Put in baking pan and dribble butter over them, then sprinkle with salt. Toast in a 350 degree oven until slightly browned. Stir occasionally so that every side is toasted. Good!

Pickled Mushrooms

2 c. white wine or
   cider vinegar
2 T. sugar
1 t. salt
2 shredded bay
   leaves
6 cloves
6 peppercorns
2 cloves garlic, sliced
2 slices lemon
1 16 oz. can large
   mushrooms

Combine vinegar, sugar, seasonings, garlic, lemon slices and mushroom liquor. Boil 3 to 4 minutes. Add mushrooms. Turn into sterilized jar and let stand in refrigerator 1 to 3 weeks.

Sauerkraut Balls

Serves 20 - 25

2 large finely
   chopped onions
1 bunch celery, finely
   chopped
3 T. butter
1 lb. ground lean
   beef
2 c. well-drained
   kraut
2 c. flour
$\frac{1}{2}$ t. salt
$\frac{1}{2}$ t. Accent
$\frac{1}{8}$ t. black pepper
2 eggs

Cook onion and celery in butter until brown. Add beef; cook over low heat about 8 minutes. Cool. Add kraut (must be very dry), flour, seasonings and unbeaten eggs. Mix thoroughly. Shape into balls 1 inch in diameter. Fry in deep fat heated to 390 degrees about 2 minutes, or until brown. Drain on absorbent paper. Serve hot.

These are so delicious and so different.

Cheese Carrots

Grate sharp yellow cheddar. Moisten it with cream or mayonnaise until it is of good consistency to handle. Shape in form of small carrots. In the blunt end, place a sprig of parsley.

Nut Cheese Balls

½ c. **Roquefort cheese, or part Roquefort and part cream cheese**
1 T. **butter**
½ t. **Lea & Perrins or 1 T. brandy**
½ t. **paprika**
A few grains of cayenne

Work to a paste. Shape into 1 inch balls. Roll them in ¼ cup ground nut meats, chopped herbs or watercress. Chill them. This is also effective made into a large cheese ball.

Deep Fried Cheese Dreams

½ lb. **grated Swiss cheese**
3 **well-beaten eggs**
1 t. **baking powder**
1 T. **sherry**
⅛ t. **paprika**

Preheat deep fryer to 375 degrees. Mix all ingredients. Put some flour in a narrow glass or cup. Drop a tablespoon of the mixture into the flour and swirl it until it is coated with flour. Fry until golden brown.

Pumpkin or Squash Blooms Fried _____

Gather blooms in the early morning while crisp. Make a batter of ½ cup flour, salt, pepper, egg, and ¼ cup milk. Dip blooms in this and fry until a golden brown.

Cheese Ball _____

8 oz. pimiento cheese (Ruth's)
8 oz. New York cheddar cheese (sharp)
8 oz. Swiss cheese
8 oz. cream cheese
Juice of 2 lemons
1 med. onion, grated
4 c. chopped pecans
½ to ¾ t. red pepper
½ t. salt
½ t. pepper

Blend all ingredients and shape into a ball.

Here are two good dessert ideas for parties:

_____

Lemon Water Ice _____ Serves 12

3 c. water
2 c. sugar
2 c. strained lemon
  juice
2 T. grated lemon
  rind
Mint sprigs

Combine water and sugar in a saucepan and bring to a boil. Simmer 5 minutes and cool. Add lemon juice and rind. Pour the mixture into a freezer tray and freeze. When preparing to serve, shave the mixture by scraping the surface with a heavy spoon. Spoon into sherbet dishes and return to freezer until ready to serve. Garnish with sprigs of mint.

Peanut Butter Custard _____ Serves 6

1 c. peanut butter
4½ oz. custard
  dessert mix
4 c. milk

Combine peanut butter and dessert mix; gradually add milk, stirring until smooth. Cook over medium heat, stirring constantly until custard comes to a full boil. Pour into container and let stand 2 minutes. Place waxed paper directly on top of custard. Refrigerate at least 1 hour.

Other Party Ideas

For cocktails before dinner, allow only two drinks per person. One quart, which contains 32 ounces, will make 21 drinks the same size.

One rule of thumb for punches calls for 1 quart liquor (rum, vodka, bourbon), 1 quart fruit juice (any one, or a mixture), 1 quart ginger ale and 1 quart soda. Combine liquor and fruit juice, adding ginger ale and soda at serving time.

Arrange fruit or flowers in the bottom of an ice mold in thin layer of water. Freeze until fruit or flowers are anchored in place and then fill with more water and freeze. Dip quickly in warm water to unmold. Festive ice cubes may be made by adding a cherry, sprig of mint or lemon twist to each section of ice cube tray. Boil water before making cubes—this assures you of no bubbles.

Dip lemon slices in chopped parsley for garnishes.

Slip julienne carrot slices through black or green olive slices.

BREADS, PIES
AND PASTRIES

My Aunt Effie was a very colorful, beautiful lady. With her high-necked, lacy collars and her flowing skirts, she could have graced the table of the President of the United States or the Queen of England. My visits to her home were incomparable. I was treated as a member of the royalty. She brought forth delectable foods that to me are unforgettable. One is this Corn Pone.

Aunt Effie's Corn Pone

Combine 1 quart sifted cornmeal, 1 cup uncooked oats and 1 teaspoon salt. Mix with enough warm water to make a stiff dough. Let stand, covered, overnight. The next morning stir in 1 cup buttermilk, 1 teaspoon soda, ½ cup molasses and 2 well-beaten eggs. Mix thoroughly. Bake in a slow oven 2 hours or longer.

Here are some more of our favorite bread recipes:

Louise's Steamed Corn Bread

2 c. sweet milk
3 c. cornmeal
1 c. sour milk
1 t. soda
²/₃ c. molasses
1 c. flour
1 egg
1 t. salt

Mix all ingredients and pour into a greased 3 pound can. Put a few inches of water in a 4 pound lard bucket. Place the can of batter inside this bucket; place bucket on heat and cover. Steam bread by simmering 3 hours.

Jackie's Pumpkin Nut Bread

2 c. sifted flour
2 t. baking powder
¹/₂ t. soda
1 t. salt
1 t. cinnamon
¹/₂ t. nutmeg
1 c. canned solid
   pack pumpkin
1 c. sugar
¹/₂ c. milk
2 eggs
¹/₄ c. butter (softened)
1 c. pecans (chopped)

Sift together first 6 ingredients. Combine pumpkin, sugar, milk and eggs in mixing bowl. Add dry ingredients and butter. Mix until well blended. Stir in pecans.

Spread in well-greased 9 x 5 x 3 inch loaf pan. Bake in 350 degree oven for 45 to 55 minutes, or until toothpick inserted in center comes out clean.

This recipe makes 1 loaf. For 2 loaves, use 1 can (No. 303) pumpkin and double remaining ingredients. Bread may be frozen.

This recipe was given to me by Jackie Painter.

My Mother's Corn Pone

Sift about 1½ quarts cornmeal, adding the usual amount of salt as for bread, 2 tablespoons sugar and 1½ pint flour. Sift together again. Have water boiling briskly. Stir just enough boiling water into mixture to make a stiff dough. Put to cool. When heat is out of dough, stir in a package of yeast that has been dissolved in ½ cup lukewarm water. Stir well. Put dough in a warm place to rise overnight. When it is doubled in bulk, stir down and let rise again. Then stir in 1 cup buttermilk with ½ teaspoon soda dissolved in it and 1 beaten egg. Then bake slowly in a greased heavy iron kettle with a lid.

Carrot Bread

3 eggs
1½ c. oil
2 c. sugar
3 c. flour
1 t. soda
1 t. salt
3 t. cinnamon
3 t. vanilla
1 c. nuts
2 c. grated carrot
1 c. crushed
  pineapple (small
  can) with juice

Beat together well the first nine ingredients; add carrot and pineapple. Mix all ingredients well and bake in 2 large greased loaf pans. Bake at 325 degrees for 1 hour.

Gritted Bread _____ Serves 6

Just as ears of corn are beginning to harden, but when they are still in milky stage, gather early in the day. Cut off grains, then scrape enough for 2 cups. Add 1 tablespoon melted butter, 1 tablespoon cornmeal, ½ cup sweet milk, 3 well beaten eggs and salt to taste. Put in well-greased deep dish and bake in hot oven—400 degrees.

Sara Belle's Yeast Biscuits _____

1 c. warm water
2 pkgs. yeast
3 t. sugar
¾ c. cooking oil
2 c. buttermilk
1 t. soda
5 c. self-rising flour

Mix all ingredients. Roll out a portion of dough and place in 400 degree oven and bake to desired brownness. Place remainder of dough in refrigerator in a covered dish. Take out and roll out and bake at any time. Keeps for 2 weeks. This recipe makes enough dough for about 2½ dozen biscuits.

Charlotte's Very Best Rolls

1 c. cold water
1 c. hot water
2 pkgs. yeast
1 c. sugar
2 c. Crisco
1½ T. salt
4 eggs
2 c. warm water
All-purpose flour

Mix cold water, hot water and yeast. Let stand until yeast rises to top—about 40 minutes.

Mix sugar, Crisco and salt with hands, mixing thoroughly. Add eggs and mix well. Then add water. Add yeast mixture and enough flour for a good consistency (not stiff). Put in refrigerator and let stay until ready to use. Will keep a week in well-covered bowl. When ready to bake, butter hands well with melted butter. Pinch off dough and put in greased muffin tins. I use two pinches for each tin. Let rise about 1 hour. Use butter freely when pinching. Bake at 400 degrees. About 24 rolls.

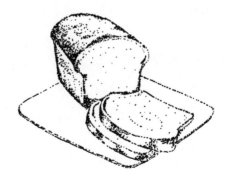

"This Is the Bread that Was!" _____ by Betty Masket

Dissolve 1¹/₂ tablespoons yeast in ¹/₂ cup lukewarm water with 2 tablespoons sugar and let stand 45 minutes. Scald 1 cup milk and add 1 cup boiling water to it. Put in ¹/₄ pound of butter so it will melt. Add ¹/₂ cup sugar and 1¹/₂ table-spoons salt and mix so the sugar and salt dissolve. When this mixture is lukewarm, add it to the yeast mixture. Beat 3 eggs and add to the above. Add about 4 cups flour a little at a time, beating after each addition. Then beat for 1 minute. Add about 4 more cups of flour and mix well after each addition—then knead until the dough does not stick to the bowl and is elastic. Grease dough all over with oil. Cover with a damp cloth and let rise until double in bulk (about 2 hours). Knead down and let rise again until double (about 1 hour). Knead; divide in 3 parts; make into loaves. Let stand 10 minutes, then put into well-greased loaf pans and let rise 1 hour. Mix an egg yolk with 2 tablespoons water and brush on top of the loaves. (You can sprinkle poppy or sesame seed on top.) Bake at 500 degrees for 10 minutes. Turn oven down to 350 degrees and bake 20 minutes. Remove from pans and cool on cake rack.

Corn Bread _____

Cook 1 cup dried apricots in a little water with 1 cup sugar. Cook slowly until thick as desired. Mix together with 2 cups sifted home-ground yellow cornmeal in mixing bowl, plus a pinch of salt; pour over this enough hot water to make a stiff dough. Place in a hot iron pan and bake under broiler until brown, then turn and brown other side.

This corn pone finger bread is so good everyone loved it cold or hot with butter. To us it was better than cake.

Sally Lunn

Cream together ½ cup butter, 1 tablespoon sugar and ½ teaspoon salt. Add 2 eggs and beat. Dissolve 1 package yeast in 1 cup lukewarm water. Add to egg mixture. Add 3 cups flour and beat to a good consistency. Pour into buttered tube cake pan. Let rise 1½ hours. Bake at 300 degrees for 45 minutes. Eat hot if possible.

Pies and Pastries

Mardel's Pie Crust

Measure 2 cups plain flour in large bowl. Add 1 teaspoon salt. To this add ½ cup oil and ¼ cup cold milk. These should be measured together in same cup. Stir with fork until all the flour is worked into oil and milk. Shape dough into a ball and place between 2 pieces of waxed paper. Pat flat with hand and then roll into a thin layer. Take off top layer of paper, pick up paper with crust on it and turn into pie pan. Peel off waxed paper. Bake in 400 degree oven. Makes 1 crust.

French Pie Pastry

3 c. flour
1½ t. salt
1½ c. shortening
1 egg
⅓ c. cold water
1 t. vinegar

Mix flour, salt and shortening. Beat egg in water, add vinegar. Add to dry ingredients and mix well with fork. Let rest 10 minutes before rolling into crusts. Yields crust for 2 double-crust or 4 single-crust pies.

Japanese Fruit Pie

1 stick margarine
1 c. sugar
2 eggs, beaten
1/2 c. macaroon
    coconut (fine)
1/2 c. pecans, chopped
    fine
1/2 c. dates
1 t. vanilla
1/2 t. vinegar

Melt margarine with sugar. Beat. Cool. Mix in other ingredients and pour into an uncooked pie crust. (Use French Pie Pastry, above.) Bake at 300 degrees until done. Bake at least 30 minutes.

Fudge Pie

1/2 c. margarine
1 c. sugar
1 sq. semi-sweet
    chocolate, melted
2 eggs
1/2 c. flour
1 t. vanilla
Vanilla ice cream or
    whipping cream

Grease a 9 inch pie pan. Cream margarine, add sugar and mix. Add chocolate. Add eggs, one at a time, beating hard after each addition. Stir in sifted flour and vanilla. Pour into the pie pan and bake for 30 minutes at 375 degrees. Cool in pan. When ready to serve, cut in wedges and serve with a scoop of ice cream or a generous amount of whipped cream.

Creates-Its-Own-Crust Coconut Pie _____

¼ c. margarine
1 c. sugar
2 eggs
1 c. milk
¼ c. self-rising flour
3½ ounces flaked
coconut

Preheat oven to 350 degrees. Cream margarine and sugar. Add eggs, one at a time, mixing well after each addition. Add milk and flour, blending well; add coconut. Pour into a lightly greased 9 inch pie pan. Bake for 40 minutes or until set.

Sister's Coconut Pie _____

1 stick margarine
(melt and set aside)
7 oz. can coconut
5 eggs
2 c. sugar
1 t. vanilla
1 c. buttermilk,
less 1 T.

Mix all ingredients together except margarine. Pour into 2 unbaked 9 inch pie shells and bake at 350 degrees for 30 minutes. Pour melted margarine over top of pies just before they are done. Makes 2 pies.

Easy Caramel Pie _____

1 large can
evaporated milk
2 eggs, beaten
1 c. brown sugar
2 heaping T. flour
1 t. vanilla
¼ t. salt

Cook all ingredients together until thick. Cool and pour in cooled baked pie shell. Top with Cool Whip or Dream Whip.

Transparent Pie

4 eggs, slightly
   beaten
1½ c. sugar
½ stick margarine
1 T. plus ½ t. vinegar
1 t. vanilla

Mix and pour into an unbaked crust. Bake at 350 degrees for 35 to 40 minutes.

Lemonade Pie

1 can Eagle Brand
   Condensed Milk
1 sm. can frozen
   lemonade
1 large carton Cool
   Whip

Mix milk and lemonade. Fold in Cool Whip. Pour in two 8 inch graham cracker crusts. Chill. Very good!

Drunken Pumpkin Pie

1 c. pumpkin
1 c. sugar
1½ c. evaporated
   milk
¼ c. bourbon
3 egg yolks
1 t. cinnamon
1 t. mace
½ t. nutmeg
3 egg whites, beaten
   stiff

Mix all ingredients except egg whites; then fold in egg whites, pour into a 9 inch unbaked pie shell and sprinkle a few pecans on top. Bake at 450 degrees for 15 minutes. Reduce heat to 300 degrees and bake 20 minutes more.

Angel Chocolate Chiffon Pie _____

First, make a meringue shell by beating until foamy: 2 egg whites, 1/8 teaspoon salt and 1/8 teaspoon cream of tartar. Add 1/2 cup sifted sugar. Beat until stiff. fold in 1/2 cup pecan pieces, chopped but not fine, and 1/2 teaspoon vanilla. Grease a 9 inch pie pan with vegetable shortening. Spread mixture in the greased pie pan, building up on the pan rim to 1/2 inch above pan. Bake at 300 degrees for 1 1/2 hours. Cool.

For the filling, melt together 2 tablespoons sugar, 1 small package semi-sweet chocolate drops and 3 tablespoons milk. Stir and cool. Separate 4 eggs. Add egg yolks one at a time, beating between each addition, to chocolate mixture. Beat egg whites until stiff. Fold chocolate mixture into egg whites. Put filling in meringue shell and chill. Top each serving with whipped cream that has been sweetened with powdered sugar.

Sister Lizzie's Shaker Pie _____

1/3 c. flour
1 c. brown sugar
1 3/4 c. light cream
1 t. vanilla
1/4 c. soft margarine
A pinch of nutmeg
9 inch unbaked pie
    shell

Mix flour and sugar. Place in bottom of pie shell. Mix cream, vanilla and soft margarine (in small pieces); pour into pie shell. Sprinkle with nutmeg over top. Bake in a 350 degree oven for 40 to 45 minutes or until firm.

Pecan Hassees

For the crust, mix ¼ pound margarine, 3 ounces cream cheese and 1 cup flour. Divide into 24 balls. Place each ball in a tiny muffin tin. Press to form a crust, covering bottom and sides.

For the filling, break up 2 eggs with a fork, but *do not beat*. Add 1½ cups firmly packed brown sugar, 2 tablespoons melted margarine, pinch of salt and 1 teaspoon vanilla. Put a few chopped nuts in bottom of each crust. Fill with the filling. Sprinkle top with chopped nuts. Bake in a 350 degree oven for 30 minutes.

Shakertown Lemon Pie

Unbaked pastry for bottom and top crusts (I use French Pie Pastry recipe)
2 lemons
2 c. sugar
4 eggs

Slice lemons, including rind, as thin as paper. Place in bowl and pour sugar over. Mix well and let stand for 2 hours or more. Beat the eggs together and pour over the lemons. Fill unbaked pie shell with mixture and put top crust on. Slit small vents in top crust. Place in a preheated 450 degree oven for 15 minutes. Cut heat down to 350 degrees and bake for 30 minutes or until a knife is inserted and comes out clean.

Southern Pecan Pie

2 c. brown sugar
 (packed)
1 c. white sugar
½ lb. margarine (2
 sticks)
6 eggs
2 c. pecans
2 unbaked pie shells
Whipped cream

Boil sugars and margarine together. Beat eggs, then blend very slowly with hot syrup as you continue to beat. Divide mixture evenly between pie shells and sprinkle with pecans. Bake in a 350 degree oven for 20 minutes and for 15 minutes at 400 degrees. Pies will crack slightly and be jelly-like. Serve with a collar of whipped cream.

Sunny Silver Pie

4 egg yolks
2 - 3 T. lemon juice
1 lemon rind, grated
⅛ t. salt
½ c. sugar
1½ t. gelatin
⅓ c. cold water
4 egg whites
½ c. sugar
1 c. whipping cream

In double boiler, combine egg yolks, lemon juice, lemon rind, salt and sugar. Cook over boiling water until thick, stirring constantly. Remove from heat. Soak gelatin in cold water and add to egg yolk mixture. Beat egg whites well with sugar and fold into egg yolk mixture. Pour into unbaked pie shell and refrigerate for 2 to 3 hours, until firm. Whip cream and spread on top of pie.

Black Bottom Pie

14 crisp gingersnaps
5 T. margarine
4 egg yolks, beaten
2 c. milk, scalded
   and kept hot
½ c. sugar
1¼ T. cornstarch
1½ sq. sweet
   chocolate, melted
1 t. vanilla
1 T. gelatin
4 T. cold water
4 egg whites
½ c. sugar
¼ t. cream of tartar
2 T. rum
1 c. whipping cream
½ sq. sweet
   chocolate

Roll gingersnaps in a paper bag until they are fine crumbs. Add margarine and pat the mixture evenly into a 9 inch pie pan. Bake 10 minutes in a 300 degree oven. Allow to cool.

To make custard, add egg yolks slowly to hot milk in a double boiler. Combine sugar and cornstarch and stir into egg yolk mixture. Cook over boiling water for 20 minutes, stirring occasionally, until mixture generously coats a spoon. Remove from heat. Take out 1 cup of this custard and place in a separate bowl. To this 1 cup of custard add the chocolate and beat well. As it cools, add vanilla, pour into gingersnap crust, and chill.

While this chocolate custard is chilling, thoroughly blend gelatin and cold water and add to remaining hot custard mixture. Let cool but not thicken.

Beat egg whites, sugar and cream of tartar into a meringue and fold into custard. Add rum. As soon as chocolate custard has set in crust, pour this custard mixture over. Chill again until set.

Whip cream and spread on top of pie. Shave chocolate and sprinkle over top.

DIET RECIPES

St. Tropez Mushrooms for Two

1 lb. mushrooms
½ c. bouillon
4 black olives,
  chopped
1 garlic clove
Salt and pepper
1 T. chopped parsley

Wash the mushrooms. Leave whole if small; if not, quarter them. Heat bouillon, add the mushrooms, olives and garlic. Cook over very low heat for 5 minutes, or until just done. Remove garlic. Season with salt and pepper; add the parsley. Serve at once.

Vinaigrette Low Calorie Dressing

1 T. cornstarch
1 c. cold water
2 T. lemon juice
2 T. salad oil
1 t. horseradish
2 T. chopped gherkin
¼ t. paprika
2 T. wine vinegar
1 t. each salt and
  sugar
1 t. mustard
1 t. Worcestershire
1 T. minced parsley

Mix cornstarch with cold water and cook over low heat, stirring, about 5 minutes until it begins to boil. Continue stirring until clear and slightly thickened. Cool, then add rest of ingredients. Beat until blended.

This keeps well in refrigerator, but it will have to be beaten or shaken before each use.

Meat Patties in Wine for Four —————————

½ lb. chopped lean
  steak
½ lb. chopped lean
  veal
2 sm. chopped
  onions
2 whole eggs
4 T. chopped parsley
Salt and pepper
1 c. red wine
2 tomatoes, sliced
4 oz. mushrooms

Carefully mix the meats with onions, eggs and ⅔ of the parsley. Season with salt and pepper. Divide this preparation into 8 equal parts and shape into oblong patties. Pour half of the wine into a small oven dish. Place the patties in the dish, tomato slices on top. Sprinkle with rest of parsley; surround with mushrooms. Pour on rest of wine. Bake in a 350 degree oven for 30 minutes. Serve very hot.

Mushroom-Shrimp Salad for Two —————————

½ lb. mushrooms
¼ lb. cooked shrimp,
  shelled and
  deveined
1 T. Vinaigrette Low
  Calorie Dressing
  (see index)

Simmer mushrooms in very, very little water, covered, for 5 to 7 minutes. Drain and slice thinly. Reserve a few of the largest shrimp; cut the others in small pieces and mix with mushrooms. Season with a tablespoon of Vinaigrette Low Calorie Dressing and garnish with large shrimp.

Baked Scallops in Shells for Two

6 large scallops
Court bouillon (clear
   broth made from
   fish)
2 crumbled crackers
¼ c. skim milk
8 large mushrooms,
   chopped
2 t. chopped parsley
1 clove garlic, minced
½ c. tomato juice

Poach scallops in court bouillon for 5 minutes. Drain and chop. Soak crackers in milk and squeeze to remove excess milk. Combine scallops and crackers with mushrooms, parsley and garlic. Fill ceramic ramekins with mixture. Pour tomato juice over surface and bake in a 400 degree oven for about 10 minutes.

Turban of Cod for Four

2 cod, about 2 lbs.
  cleaned
Court bouillon (clear
  broth made from
  fish)
Juice of 1 lemon
2 crumbled crackers
½ c. skim milk
2 egg whites, stiffly
  beaten
Salt and pepper to
  taste
2 T. margarine
1 c. tomato juice
Nutmeg
Curry powder or
  paprika

Poach the cod in court bouillon and lemon juice for about 12 minutes. When fish flakes easily with a fork, carefully remove bones and skin. Mash flesh with a fork. Soak cracker crumbs in milk and squeeze to remove excess milk, then add to mashed fish along with the 2 beaten egg whites, salt and pepper. Mix well. Grease a round mold with the margarine. Pour mixture into it to steam for about 20 minutes, or place mold in a pan containing 1 inch of hot water and bake in a 350 degree oven for 30 minutes. Serve garnished with hot tomato juice flavored with nutmeg, and either a little curry powder or a little paprika, according to preference.

Anchovy Sauce

½ pint plain yogurt
1 hard boiled egg
1 T. lemon juice
1 t. mild mustard
1 t. anchovy paste

Beat everything together. Put in refrigerator for several hours. Serve well chilled.

Sweetbreads on Skewers for Four _____

1 lb. veal
   sweetbreads
4 very thin slices
   bacon
Salt and pepper

Carefully prepare the sweetbreads; cover with water and allow to simmer gently for 20 minutes. Cut bacon into 1 inch squares and the sweetbreads into larger pieces. Season with salt and pepper. Place pieces of sweetbread and bacon alternately on 4 different skewers. Broil for 10 minutes. Serve hot.

Stuffed Celery for Two _____

2 stalks celery
4 black olives,
   chopped fine
2 T. cottage cheese
1 pinch cayenne
   pepper
1 pinch salt

Wash and dry celery. Stuff each stalk with blended olives and cheese. Sprinkle with cayenne pepper and salt. Serve cold.

Calf Liver with Herbs for Two _____

½ c. white wine
½ c. tomato juice
Chopped parsley,
   chopped scallions,
   chervil
Salt and pepper
12 oz. calf liver

Mix wine, tomato juice, herbs and salt and pepper in a pan. Put to heat and reduce for about 10 minutes. Then put the liver in the pan, turning once or twice until liver loses its color. Cook over medium heat, covering the pan the last 2 or 3 minutes before serving.

Cottage Cheese with Herbs

Chop carefully assorted herbs (parsley, chervil, chives, tarragon, etc.) and mix them with 2 tablespoons cottage cheese. Add the yolk of 1 hard boiled egg. Spread on crisp bread and decorate with 3 capers each.

Crab Indian for Two

2 crabs (to yield about ¾ lb. crabmeat)
Court bouillon (clear broth made from fish)
2 T. tomato pureé
Pinch cayenne
Pinch curry powder

Cook crabs in court bouillon. Remove crabmeat carefully and chop; reserve shell. Pound the crab livers (yellow substance) and mix with tomato purée. Combine with crabmeat and add cayenne and curry powder to taste. Fill crab shells and bake in a 450 degree oven for 10 minutes.

Stewed Apples with Apricots for Two

2 good sized apples
½ c. dried apricots soaked in ½ c. water
Several drops lemon juice
1 pinch cinnamon
1 pinch grated lemon rind

Cut apples in little pieces without peeling. Put in saucepan with apricots, lemon juice, cinnamon and lemon rind. Cover and cook slowly for ½ hour. Remove 2 apricot halves and put the rest of the mixture through a sieve. Pour into two bowls and serve cold. Garnish with reserved apricot halves.

Scallops in White Wine for Two

¹/₂ c. white wine
6 scallops
2 onions, chopped
1 clove garlic, minced
Salt and pepper
Cracker crumbs
2 T. chopped parsley

Pour wine into small baking dish and add scallops. Cover with onions and garlic. Sprinkle with salt and pepper and cracker crumbs. Bake in a 400 degree oven for 10 minutes. Garnish with chopped parsley and serve at once.

HINTS FOR
HOME AND GARDEN

Do you know how to make a jelly test? It is more easily done than described, but, roughly, it goes like this: After the jelly is boiling hard, use the cooking spoon with which you are stirring it to take up a little of the mix; wave the spoon around over the kettle until the juice cools slightly, then pour it back into the pot. If it runs off the spoon like water, the jelly is nowhere near ready. If it drips off the spoon in two places, it is approaching the jelly point. When the last two drops run together, sheet off the spoon and seem to break at the edge of the spoon when they drop, snatch the jelly from the fire. This sounds difficult, but go ahead and try it, for you will soon master the art.

If you add a little milk to water in which cauliflower is cooking, the cauliflower will remain attractively white.

To preserve leftover egg yolks for future use, place them in a small bowl and add 2 tablespoons cooking oil. Put in refrigerator. The yolks will remain soft and fresh.

When cooking cabbage, place a small tin cup half full of vinegar on the stove near the cabbage, and this will absorb all odor from it.

A clean clothespin provides a cool handle to steady the cake tin when removing hot cake.

Try using a thread instead of a knife when a cake is to be cut while hot.

To keep egg yolks from crumbling when slicing hard-cooked eggs, wet the knife before each cut.

Whether you cook in water, pan, double boiler, or in the oven, moderate heat prevents toughness in eggs.

If you have a garden, pick your green corn just before meal time and try cooking in milk. It's yum yum!

To remove skins from tomatoes, put in hot water or hold over flame. Remove skins, place in refrigerator to become firm for slicing.

When possible, cook vegetables and fruits in their "jackets" as most of the food value is contained in these skins.

To sour a cup of sweet milk quickly, add 2 tablespoons lemon juice.

To get a better flavor and natural sweetness from cooked fruits, serve while hot.

The connoisseur will tell you that you can never experience the true flavor of coffee when you add sugar and cream.

Never boil coffee after it has been made.

An empty stomach is not conducive to beauty.

There is no true economy in "substitutes."

Canned fruit juices may be used as a substitute for sugar in beverages, sauces or other fruits.

Few are the cooks who can view their results impartially.

Things that do not mix—alcohol and gasoline, cigarettes and linen tablecloths.

A guest helper in your kitchen usually succeeds in spoiling your good efforts.

Have you ever tried a few drops of Worcestershire sauce on bacon before broiling? It does things to it.

Beef is the juiciest of all roasts, its juice the tastiest. When simply seasoned, very little water added, it is mighty good.

When flavoring all kinds of fish, meats and vegetables, nothing excels good fresh butter.

Cooked poultry meat should be eaten promptly. Leftovers should be stored in the coldest part of the refrigerator.

It is a great mistake for an amateur cook to try to master too many dishes. It is much better to strive for excellence in a few.

Some serve the salad as a separate course, but I believe it

should be served before the entrée unless the salad is the principal dish.

The hardest dish to sidestep is something "I made especially for you."

Roll lemons, oranges and grapefruit firmly on countertop before cutting, if you want to extract more juice.

Remember, to be a good cook, you must know when to put it on and when to take if off.

When an unbaked pie crust is to be filled with a very moist filling, it is best to brush its surface with a small amount of lightly beaten egg white, then chill crust.

Peel a cucumber. Remove seeds and fill with cheese. Chill and cut crosswise.

If you have over-salted soup, dilute with water or milk if the stock is strong enough to stand thinning. If not, cook slices of potatoes in it and then throw them away—they absorb the salt.

To tell if a custard is done, dip a silver spoon into mixture. If the custard forms a straight line across the spoon, the custard should be removed from the stove. If the line is wavy, the custard is not done.

Rules of thumb for good cooking: Use little water lightly salted—cook a short time—and never add soda to cooking water.

Have water boiling when you put green vegetables on to cook.

Leaving the lid off helps green vegetables to keep the bright green color. With leafy vegetables such as greens, use lid at start until they are wilted.

Serve all the juice with the cooked vegetables or use it in soup or sauce. That's being thrifty with vitamins.

When using butter for sandwiches, it should be whipped. You may add whipped cream, 1 cup to 1 pound margarine. For zest add lemon juice, onion juice, garlic, thyme or mustard, but use them sparingly.

Putting chopped onions in cold water before using takes out the sting and often improves their flavor.

To whiten laces, wash them in sour milk.

To keep handkerchiefs, socks or other small pieces from wrapping around washing machine wringers, fold them in a towel and run through.

If you have a new broom, dip it in hot salt water before using. This will toughen the straw and make it last longer.

To remove burned-on starch from your iron, sprinkle salt on a sheet of waxed paper and slide iron back and forth over salt several times. Then polish iron with silver polish until roughness or stain is removed.

In removing stains, the fabric used and the stain should be carefully analyzed. So many of the synthetics cannot be treated as cottons and wools. Acid can be neutralized with a weak alkali such as ammonia or baking soda. Test for neutralization with litmus paper. Apply paper to wet stain. Acids will turn paper red, alkalies will turn it blue. If the stain has been neutralized, the paper won't change color.

Cottons and linens are not affected by diluted alkalies. Strong solutions cause the fabrics to turn yellow. Wool and silk are weakened by strong alkali solutions and if too-strong alkali is used, the fabrics may be destroyed.

If the material has been stained with a mild alkali such as ammonia or washing soda, and it is washable, rinse it quickly and thoroughly in lukewarm water.

If you wish to restore original color, a mild acid such as vinegar, lemon juice or 10 percent solution of acetic acid may be used.

To remove blood stains if the material is washable, soak in cold water until the stain turns light brown. Then wash in warm soapy water. Rinse thoroughly. It may be necessary to boil some blood stains if they are not removed by above method.

To remove coffee or tea stains, soak in cold water. Wash in lukewarm soapy water. Rinse thoroughly.

Grass stains are easily removed in a hot water and mild soap washing.

To remove iron rust if material is washable, stretch the

stained portion over a kettle of boiling water. Squeeze lemon juice on the stain. Let stand a few minutes. Rinse the material thoroughly in lukewarm water. Repeat if necessary, using a lukewarm water.

MENU TERMS

This is a list of menu terms we found essential for us to know as innkeepers. It is good to acquaint yourself with these if you plan any travels:

à la (ah lah): after the style or fashion.

à la broche (ah lah brosh): cooked on a skewer.

à la carte (ah lah cart'): foods prepared to order and priced separately.

à la française (ah lah frahn sayz'): in the French manner.

à la mode: in the United States, used to mean desserts are served topped with ice cream.

à la Newburg: served in a rich wine sauce of egg yolk and cream, flavored with shrimp.

à la Normande: dish with apples and fish.

ambrosia (am bro' zhia): cold dessert of bananas, shredded coconut and oranges.

anchovy (an cho' vee): small fish of the herring family.

anglaise (on glaze') *sauce*: béchamel with smothered onions, highly seasoned.

antipasto (an tee pah'stoh): mixture made of tuna fish, mushrooms and pimiento.

aspic (as' pik): clear meat, poultry or tomato jelly.

au beurre roux (oh ber roo'): with browned butter.

au gratin (oh grah' tin): a term applied to certain dishes prepared with sauce, bread crumbs and cheese, then baked.

au jus (oh ju'): served with natural juices or gravy.

au naturel (oh nah tu rel'): plainly cooked.

baked alaska: brick ice cream on cake, covered with meringue and oven-browned quickly.

Bavarian cream: gelatin, cream and egg, as dessert.

béchamel (bay' sha mel): white sauce seasoned with onion, spices and carrots.

bill of fare: the menu; list of food dishes.

bisque (bisk): a rich cream soup usually of shellfish; also a frozen whipped cream dessert with nuts.

bordelaise (bor de layz'): white or brown sauce containing onions, carrots, celery, thyme, butter and bay leaves.

borscht (borch): Russian soup made of beef stock, beets, tomatoes, eggs, sugar and seasoning.

Boston cream pie: a two-layered sponge cake with thick custard filling.

bouillabaisse (bwoo ya bace'): five or six varieties of fish, cooked together with white wine.

brochette (bro shet'): meat broiled on a skewer.

brown betty: apple pudding with bread crumbs and spices.

Brunswick stew: Traditional Southern stew, made of veal or chicken with corn, onion, salt pork, tomatoes, potatoes and beans. Often served with barbecue.

café noir (nwahr): clear black coffee.

Camembert (cah' mehm bare): soft, full-flavored cheese.

canapé (kan a pay'): an appetizer made of fried or toasted bread spread with anchovies or other small, savory foods.

capers: flower buds and young berries of European caper which are picked and used as an ingredient of sauces, salad dressing, etc. (See the index for how to make your own.)

carte du jour (kahrt du joor): menu of the day.

caviar: eggs of sturgeon, salted and pressed; fish eggs.

charlotte russe: thin sponge cake or split lady fingers with sweetened, flavored whipped cream.

chateaubriand (sha toh bree ahn'): thick, tenderloin steak served with brown or Spanish sauces, garnished with parsley.

cheddar cheese: hard, sharp, smooth American cheese.

chive: small onion.

chutney: a relish, sweet or sour, of fruit or vegetables.

cocktail: an appetizer; may be juices, solid fruit, shellfish or alcoholic beverage.

colbert (kol bear'): meat stock or glaze with butter, wine and parsley.

compote: fruit stewed in syrup.

consommé (kon so may'): a light colored, clear soup made of meat stock.

corned beef: neck or navel pickled in brine.

cottage pudding: baked pudding of milk, butter, sugar, egg; hot sauce over all.

court bouillon: a clear broth made from fish.

creole (kray' ol) *sauce*: sauce prepared with green peppers, tomatoes and onions; soup and fish *à la creole* are prepared with these ingredients.

crêpe suzette (krape su zette'): thin, fried pancake, rolled and served with a rich sauce. Usually flamed with liquor.

croquettes (kro kets'): mixture of chopped and cooked foods, shaped, rolled in bread crumbs and fried in deep fat.

croutons (kroo' tons): small cubes of fried or toasted bread served with soup.

curry: a highly spiced yellow powder, used as a seasoning.

cutlet: a small piece of meat, usually veal cut from leg for broiling or frying; or a mixture, usually of fish, shaped and cooked like a meat cutlet.

deep dish pie: a fruit pie, with top crust only, baked in a deep dish.

demitasse: small cup of strong, black coffee, served without cream or sugar.

deviled: highly seasoned; chopped or ground and mixed.

drawn butter: melted butter. Drawn butter sauce: butter, flour and salt.

éclair (e klare'): a small oblong pastry filled with custard or whipped cream and iced.

Edam (e'dam): red ball of hard, rubbery Dutch cheese.

en brochette (ahn broh shet'): cooked on a skewer.

en casserole: served in the dish in which it is baked.

en tasse (ahn tahs'): served in a cup.

entrée (ahn' tray): meat dish served before the roast or main meat course. As commonly used in restaurants, may include all main dishes.

espagnole (ess pahn yohl): a brown sauce of butter, flour and meat juice.

filet mignon (fee' lay me nyon'): tenderloin of beef.

fillet (fee' lay): a boneless loin cut of beef, veal, mutton or pork, or a boneless strip of fish.

Florentine eggs: eggs baked with spinach, grated cheese, cream sauce and seasoning.

frappé (frah pay'): partly frozen water ice.

fricassee (free' kah say): poultry, veal or lamb cut up, stewed and served with white sauce.

glaze: stock boiled down to the thickness of jelly and used to improve the appearance and flavor of braised dishes.

goulash: Hungarian: chunks of beef simmered with onions, paprika and other seasonings.

grenadine (gre nah deen'): syrup of pomegranates or red currants used in various mixed drinks.

gumbo: soup of meat, okra, tomatoes, green peppers and seasoning.

hollandaise sauce: yellow sauce made with yolk of egg, butter and lemon juice.

hors d'oeuvres (or durv'): appetizers.

Indian pudding: dessert made of cornmeal, milk, brown sugar, eggs, raisins and seasoning. Bake slowly.

Irish stew: lamb, dumplings, carrots, turnips, potatoes, onions and seasoning.

italienne (ee tah lee en'): rich brown sauce made from mushrooms, truffles, ham, tomatoes and flavoring herbs. Also, garnish with macaroni croquettes and artichoke bottoms fried in oil.

jambalaya (jam ba la' ya): rice with onions, tomatoes and shrimp.

julienne (zhu lee en'): vegetables cut in long slices thinner than French fried and served very crisp.

Limburger: soft, rich, odorous cheese.

maitre d'hôtel (mai tre doh tel'): head of catering department; head of food service.

meringue chantilly (meh rayng' shahn til ee): meringue shells stuffed with whipped cream.

milanaise: spaghetti or macaroni served with tomato sauce or a pink sauce made of white sauce and tomato.

mock turtle soup: veal, calf's head, spices.

mongol soup: tomatoes, split peas, julienne vegetables.

mongolese soup: beef extract, cheese, vegetables and spaghetti.

mornay (mor nay'): béchamel with mushroom sauce, cream and Parmesan cheese.

mousse (moos): frozen dessert of whipped cream, flavoring and sweetening.

mulligatawny (mull ee ga taw' nee) *soup*: veal, onions, carrots, tomatoes, peppers, curry powder.

neapolitan ice cream: bricks in three colors or flavors.

nesselrode (nes sel rode'): a frozen pudding of chestnuts, fruit and cream.

o'brien: with green pepper.

oeuf (uf): egg.

parfait (par fay'): frozen dessert of syrup, beaten eggs, whipped cream and flavoring.

peach melba: ice cream on half peach, with raspberry sauce.

petit fours (pe tee foor'): small cakes.

piquant (pe kant'): flavored, highly seasoned.

poulet (poo lay'): chicken.

praline (pra' lene): southern candy of pecans, maple sugar or syrup, and cream.

prime ribs: forequarter of beef; last six ribs.

provincial: prepared with a gravy made of herbs, shallots, mushrooms and meat stock.

purée (pu ray'): pulp or paste of vegetable or fruit; also thick soup.

ragout (rah goo'): thick savory stew of highly seasoned meat.

ravioli (ra vyo' li): Italian baked main dish of flour, egg, cheese, chicken stock, spinach and tomatoes.

rissolée (ree soh lay'): browned.

Rockefeller: oysters on half shell with sauce of onion, celery, bread and seasonings, browned on a bed of rock salt under a flame.

Roquefort cheese (roke' furt): semi-hard, white, crumbly, streaked with green mold.

Roquefort dressing: French dressing with Roquefort cheese and onion sauce.

Russian dressing: mayonnaise, lemon juice, chili sauce, Worcestershire and chopped pimiento.

Scotch broth: lamb or mutton, barley, carrots, onions, etc.

spumone (spoo mo' nay): chilled Italian pudding of custard variety.

squab: a young pigeon.

supreme: white sauce; broth and thin cream.

table d'hôte (tahbl doht'): fixed-price meal.

tartar sauce: mayonnaise beaten with green onions, chives and sour pickles.

timbale: shell of pastry made on a mold.

tutti frutti: mixture of fruit and nuts.

vinaigrette sauce: oil, herbs, vinegar, chopped hard-boiled eggs and pickles.

Welsh rabbit: cooked cheese, butter, beer, eggs, flavored with Worcestershire sauce and spices.

wiener schnitzel (vee' ner schnet zel): breaded veal cutlet served with anchovy fillet and slice of lemon; *à la holstein* with poached egg on top.

GARDEN HINTS

Rabbit Repellent

For years we lost all our green beans and sweet potato plants to the rabbits. So we had to do something if we were to grow them. We sprayed the leaves with water, then sprinkled red pepper on them. It did not take long for the rabbits to get the message. They left the plants alone.

Commercial Rabbit Repellent

Burpee's Seed Company has a small can, about half a pint,

of Rabbit Repellent. It is inexpensive. We used it on anything in the garden they had a taste for. It is named "Rabbit Rid." A small can lasted for two seasons and we had a large garden.

Baitless Groundhog Trap

The groundhog is most destructive. We soon found their road to the garden. They came out of the woods looking for an opening in the fence. Finding no opening, they simply dug under it. So we put a box trap flush against the fence with the opening facing the oncoming groundhogs. The curious groundhogs just walked into the trap, even when it was not baited. It sounds crazy, but it's worth a try. We caught 16 groundhogs, two opossums and a racoon in one summer.

Green Onion Tip

When putting out onion sets for green onions, plant them extra deep and you will have a lot more white stem to eat.

Fall Fertilizer Stockpile

After you have finished your yard work, place grass clippings and leaves that you have raked in a pile. In the fall, scatter the grass and leaves on your garden and turn under. It makes a great fertilizer for the next growing season.

Coffee Can Plant Feeder

My suggestion for help in growing vegetables is to use one pound coffee cans with plastic lids. First put about 10 holes in the bottom of the can. Then put them in the ground level with the surface and fill them with fertilizer, which will slowly seep into the ground and feed the plant roots.

Unbeatable Beet

Large vegetables aren't always considered of prime quality unless their strain naturally grows large. We found this true in the case of German Lutz Beets. We grew a five pound bulb that was so sweet and not a hint of toughness. This variety can be ordered from Nichols Herbs and Rare Seeds.

Battling Bugs with Lime

A sack of white lime did wonders in our garden as a bug killer. We sprinkle potato plants, corn and most other plants to keep bugs away. Also, I found that it is good in getting rid of ants. Take some lime and just sprinkle it in a circle around the ant hills. It gets rid of ants just as well as expensive ant powder.

Sunflower Companions

Here is an idea for growing pole beans in spring. Plant them alternately with giant sunflowers and forget the necessity of erecting poles for the beans, which can be easily trained to climb the sunflowers. You will enjoy the flowers and the birds will enjoy eating the seeds.

Pea/Corn Succession

We planted our peas as early as possible and cultivated as often as necessary to control weeds. When the peas began to bloom, we planted an early variety of sweet corn beside each row of peas. As soon as the peas were all harvested, we pulled out the pea vines and we had a nicely started sweet corn crop coming in. It worked fine for us and gave us two crops on the same garden space.

Growing Asparagus

We always found it hard to cultivate asparagus. We felt the plowing or hoeing cut and injured the root system. We learned to put a goodly amount of salt in the asparagus rows and around the plants. They are the one plant that likes salt. Nothing else will grow in the salt. Just fertilize well and you can forget all but gathering it as it comes in.

EPILOGUE

Names mean nothing to some people, but as the sunset of our lives grew nearer, nothing could take away the beauty of the name given to our home nor the way it had played such a part in our lives. As we looked at the sunset, the shadows of coming darkness were falling around us. We saw the evening hang a silver, then a golden crescent on the brow of night. We had watched the glory of dawn and the sleepy twilight.

We had stood there in wintertime and had listened to the ice-laden winds, and had watched the snowflakes glistening in the moonlight. We had felt and watched the gentle rains in springtime. Then, too, we had watched the storm clouds gather, and Ed had taught me to watch and appreciate the lightning followed by blasts of thunder.

Surely if there were ever an Eden it offered no more than the grandeur of the Great Smoky Mountains from the lawn of our beloved Sunset Farms.

Many of our friends and relatives visit foreign lands and see the great masterpieces which have been spread on canvas. Yet, had they stood where we stood, they could have seen a picture painted by that unseen mystic hand. We saw where the sun shines, the moon beams, the spring bubbles, the cascade sparkles, the flower blooms, the wind moans, and the bird sings. As we stood there where we had spent our happy former years, it was like a fleeting dream. But our souls were filled with sadness as we talked of time and the changes it had brought.

It was then Ed suggested to me that we must part with all this. It was really the sunset of our lives.

So before we had time to give it a second thought, Ed put our Sunset Farms on the market. And before we had time to change our minds, we were visited by a realtor and a lovely couple. They were immediately sold on our place.

I could find no pleasure in house hunting. I believed that the old house was my first and only love. But I realized we had reached a special time in life. It was time to rest. So as quickly as we sold Sunset Farms, we bought a house to live in until we could build a home of our own.

This home has a view of the Great Smokies and one of our beautiful Blue Ridges. Again we are happy!

One day we received a call from the owners of Sunset Farms to come to dinner. You may have some idea of how I felt when I imagined going as a guest, back to what had been my beloved home. It was with a feeling of nostalgia that we accepted.

It was mid-December. I had so many fond memories of this time of year.

We shall never forget the graciousness and hospitality with which we were received. Never have we been served with more grandeur, more hospitality and more elegant food.

Much had changed in decor and surroundings. The house was beautifully decorated for the season. As I recall, even the front door had the loveliest wreath, all in gold. There was a bar with anything anyone would wish to drink, and on the coffee table was a beautiful Christmas tree made of the largest, pinkest shrimp, and three or four kinds of dips to eat with the shrimp!

The crystal was Bowknot. The flatware was plain gold. The lovely lace tablecloth draped to the floor. This was our first experience in eating from gold dishes. These dishes, I later learned, had belonged to Marie Dressler and were really antiques from the Baltic region.

After bidding our gracious hosts adieu, we left with the feeling that Sunset Farms was again in the hands of people who found peace and solace in this beautiful setting. We knew that as long as they had it, it would have the greatest of love and care.

Index